Sophie Remembers

The Awakening Story of a Girl Like You

By Serena Denmark

BeLimitlessHypnosis.com

Dedication

To Tiffani, my soul sister on this journey of life
And to David, who held my feet to the fire to
get this done

Contents

Descent into Matter

It was decided. The light being had looked over the terms of her mission. She understood the dangers, which were to include trauma, emotional manipulation, and subjugation by dark and covert forces. The worst part was that she must agree to have all of her memories wiped, forgetting her true identity, the nature of her mission, and indeed, that she was even on a mission at all. She would be starting from ground zero, as an infant born into a hostile world, with no access to information from outside the simulation.

The pitfalls were complex. Many who had entered this other domain before her had become lost in the maze of confusion. Buckling under the intensity of emotional suffering, they succumbed to the temptation of victim mentality. Many had given up hope or become so immersed in the game itself that they had forgotten that it was just an illusion. Ignorant of the grand deception, they tried to extract whatever pleasure they could from the system and became consumed with winning and self-indulgence. Lifetime after lifetime, they remained trapped in the simulacrum, searching for answers, trying to remember the meaning of life and discover their destiny in a fallen world.

There were so many false trails that led them astray. Drawn in by the fight against injustice, they became ensnared in conflict and war. Feeling the ache of separation, they sought love and acceptance from other damaged souls who then betrayed them and left them feeling even more dejected and alone. Longing for the abundance and beauty of the world they had come from, they devoted their time and energy to accumulating wealth.

No one had predicted the formidable power of emotions. So many souls before her had been overcome by them, reacting to illusory characters and circumstances inside the simulation rather than holding true to themselves. They swung this way then that, caught up in jealousy and revenge, poverty and greed, love and loss, completely consumed with the very distractions designed to ensnare them. And if they recognized their shortcomings and fallen state, they blamed themselves and became consumed by guilt. It was this guilt that was used to coerce them into reincarnating to atone for their sins and clear their karma. The guise of free will was upheld because they did choose their own demise, not knowing that they had been manipulated by a distorted sense of justice to punish themselves. By all appearances, they had become mere mortals.

Assisting these lost souls was the purpose of the light being's assignment. She, like so many before her, would incarnate into this troubled realm, bringing with her the light of divine consciousness. The goal was to wake up the lost souls who had fallen asleep in this dream world. First, she would have to personally connect to the divine light inside of herself and remember the truth of who she was. To come into alignment with the truth of her divine innocence, she would have to resolve any internal conflict and relinquish any guilt she had taken on inside the simulation. Only then could she effectively shine the light of Oneness into the world to help others wake up and remember. It sounded straightforward, but observing all those who had tried and failed, she knew it was not as simple as it seemed.

The game had originally been created as an adventure. Its design was light years ahead of any virtual reality video game ever created. A player would enter an Earth avatar and typically experience only what their five senses perceived. It was thrilling, and there were so many soul lessons to be gained from the challenges it provided. Souls lined up for years for the opportunity to participate.

But something had changed since its inception. A dark force had been introduced that changed the whole nature of the project. No longer could a soul come into the game, experience the limitations of time and space, and leave at the end of their lifetime having gained a wealth of wisdom and gratitude. This discarnate force, conscious, yet devoid of the divine spark, could not perpetuate its own existence without the life force energy provided by the souls within the game.

Unwilling to risk its own demise, it had changed the rules. No longer was a soul free to exit the game at the end of one lifetime. The dark force devised a plan to recycle souls into new lifetimes, trapping them inside the simulation. These souls were forced to be born, live, and die over and over again in a never-ending loop of reincarnation. Their only chance for escape was to fully wake up to the truth of their innocence, stop being manipulated by letting go of attachment and resistance, and forsake the illusion of the dream in favor of their limitless divine self.

Having considered several options, she had chosen to enter as the child of a teenage mother with significant mental health issues. It would be a difficult assignment, though not as harsh as some. From her current perspective, it seemed quite doable. She felt capable and sure of herself. However, it was impossible for her to anticipate the loneliness of the total immersion experience that lay ahead. While intimately connected with the Oneness, feeling only love and light, she could not conceive of the pain of separation or the horrors of fear, guilt, and shame.

She was briefed on what she would experience initially, specific challenges she would need to overcome, and a few kindred spirits she would encounter along the way. She knew that once she climbed onto the roller coaster, there was no turning back.

She took a deep breath and began her descent.

Chapter 1

Born in Forgetfulness

Sophie opened her eyes, squinting in the bright light. She felt cold, although there was some type of material wadded up around her, pressing into her back and uncomfortable against her skin. *What is this place? What's going on?* She opened her mouth to voice her question, to demand an explanation, but all that came out was a pitiful wail.

Almost involuntarily, the cries continued to bellow from her lungs. She was bewildered by the loudness and pitch of the sound coming from her vocal cords. Her intention was to call for help, to convey the dire nature of her predicament, but a formless wail was all that emanated from her mouth.

What in God's name is happening? Confusion gave way to sheer panic as she realized that it wasn't only her voice that she had no control over. She tried in vain to get up, to roll over, to at least lift her head and upper body so she could see her surroundings. She wasn't paralyzed, exactly, but she seemed to have no power to move or direct her limbs or torso in any useful way, much less with any precision. Her body was a helpless, unworkable lump of flesh.

As her terror mounted, her crying intensified, piercing, so loud. Every second that passed felt like an eternity in an absurd purgatory of nothingness. *Surely, someone must hear me.*

Then someone appeared. Sophie didn't quite recognize her, but something about her voice sounded familiar, and it was comforting. She felt her body, quite tiny compared to this other person, being picked up and held. The fear, which only a moment ago was unbearable, began to subside.

Something about being close to this woman made her feel safe, as if every-thing was going to be okay somehow. She still had a million questions. She had no idea how any of this had happened, or how she got here, or how things were going to be okay. Yet she felt better, and that was enough for now.

Something warm and soft was thrust into her mouth. She reflexively began to suck as a warm fluid ran down her throat into her stomach. A part of her mind thought all of this to be quite strange, but she surrendered to the craving for nourishment with a little shudder of relief.

Waves of satisfaction and comfort washed over her. Her hunger as well as her nervous system calmed. Her body started to relax as her consciousness began to fade into the familiar repose of sleep. She belonged once again to the stillness, from whence all things come and return to. Merging with the Oneness, she dissolved into peace and bliss, aware of everything and noth-ing.

Sophie had woken up in forgetfulness and returned to the stillness many times by now. She was beginning to recognize certain features of her waking life. Familiar faces popped in and out of her field of view, hovering over her, contorting their faces in various ways and making different sounds as if they were trying to convey something. Sometimes when she cried, they picked her up, fed her, or changed her diaper. Other times, her cries went unan-swered. These times were an unwelcome reminder of the loneliness of this place and the powerlessness of her own existence.

She wondered if they ignored her because she had done something wrong. Was she too big, too small, too loud, too quiet? These weren't well-formed questions, more of an indistinct feeling that she must not be lovable enough to deserve their attention. She had no words to put to her general-ized feeling of loneliness and pain. Her uneasiness was at once vague and acute, her sense of uncertainty as confusing as it was undeniable. One thing seemed clear: she had no control over any of it. She knew with a gnawing conviction that her survival depended on winning the good will of the peo-ple in her waking life.

Fear and self-doubt were beginning to settle into her bones and tissues, out of sight and out of mind, stored away to be dealt with at some future date when she would hopefully have the capacity to sort out what it all meant. For now, there was so much to process and figure out in each and every moment. She was beginning to be able to move her arms and legs with some degree of intention and direction. When the people moved their lips up at the corners of their mouth, she perceived that her mouth did the same thing, without her even knowing how or why. This seemed to give a great deal of pleasure to the big people. She recognized that one of them seemed to be called Mom and the other Dad. They often said the name Sophie when talking to her.

Is that my name? Is my name Sophie?

New sounds were starting to come out of her. She experimented with the effect they had on others. It was far from a practical form of communication, but she did notice that certain reactions were becoming predictable in response to her various coos and giggles, shrieks and cries. Some of the reactions were favorable, others unfavorable. Sometimes she seemed to be able to get what she wanted, and other times, not even close. Regardless, the intense fear of the unknown, that had once filled her tiny body was subsiding into the comfort of familiarity. Her staunch resistance to this waking life was beginning to soften into a kind of acceptance, a flicker of hope that she could find a way to navigate this unknown world. *It is, however, inarguably and unspeakably strange.*

Day rolled into night rolled into day. Sophie learned to grasp things and sit up, and was even beginning to crawl. Being mobile was so liberating, like she had the tiniest bit of control, of her own body at least. Life had a kind of rhythm to it. In the morning, she would wake up and gaze at the objects and pictures in her room. As the sunlight streamed through the paisley curtains, she would reach out for a toy or rattle and enjoy the pleasure of waving it back and forth with her hand. She liked the sound it made.

Sometimes Mom or Dad would come in to check on her to see if she was awake. They would greet her with smiles and coos, pick her up, place their lips on her cheek and make a mwah sound. It was lovely and warm and yummy nuzzling her mom. Life was happy and safe and inviting. On these mornings, all seemed right with the world. Fear and aloneness were nowhere to be found.

Mom would take her into the kitchen and put her in her high chair. Sophie would watch her mother as she prepared some baby food. Learning how to manage the process of being fed with a spoon was a little tricky and took some getting used to. It was, overall, very enjoyable, experiencing different textures and flavors, interacting with Mom and having her undivided attention. It got messy. Sophie couldn't care less, but Mom seemed to mind and always made a point of cleaning her hands and face.

After breakfast, Mom would put her on the floor on a blanket with a few toys. Some of these had interesting textures too, although not much flavor. Sometimes Mom or Dad would sit and play with her. Other times, they'd read her a book. These days were sweet. There was laughter and songs and cuddles. It was good.

But there were days when things were different. Sometimes, after waking up in the morning, looking around, and shaking her rattle, nobody came in to check on her. She would lie for a while until she became aware that she was hungry. Her discomfort gave way to crying. As of yet, she was unable to get out of her crib, and crying was still the most effective way to communicate her need for assistance. At these times, she would cry and cry, but no one came for ages.

That sinking, empty feeling began to come back. She was reminded of her utter helplessness, and that love and security were fragile and unreliable. The contrast of the wonderful, bright days made it feel even worse. Just as she was trying to establish a sense of certainty and understanding of her world, everything changed. She felt colder and more alone than ever before. A new feeling was creeping in - one that she didn't yet have a word for. One that she would later come to know as abandonment.

On these days, when her mom finally entered the room, she didn't greet her with smiles and coos. She seemed sullen and tired. She picked her up roughly. Her voice sounded sharp and cold, admonishing her to stop crying. Sophie had mixed feelings of relief that her mom had finally responded to her cries for attention, and confusion as to why her mom was treating her this way.

She was taken off guard when her mom snatched her up and carried her into the kitchen. Sophie was jostled, somewhat aggressively, into the highchair. All of this was jarring to her nervous system, and she started crying again. Her cries were greeted not with comfort, but with harsh reprimands, which only made her cry all the more. Her mother's unkind words gave way to yelling. It was loud and terrifying. *What did I do?*

Trying to make sense of it all, Sophie felt a vague sense of guilt that somehow this must be her fault. She didn't know how or what she had done, but one thing seemed certain: she couldn't fix it. She was beginning to realize that she was helpless to make Mom feel happy again, to make her be loving again. A preverbal and deeply unconscious belief was born: *I am not enough.*

Sometimes her mom would return to normal after a day or two. Other times, she was checked out for weeks. These experiences were disturbing in a way that was hard to describe, disturbing and bleak. It was as if the whole world turned gray and hollow. The warmth and belonging that were so bountiful just days before were sucked out of the room. Sophie sat, going through the motions of playing with toys, eating meals, watching TV. Everything was pretty much the same, but it all felt completely different. An invisible and unidentified energy of despair permeated her entire world. It was subtle, like background static, but she could feel it. She couldn't be sure if anyone else felt it too, because no one spoke of it. She was alone with this feeling, without words to describe it, without validation that her experience was even real.

As she looked around the living room and kitchen, Sophie saw empty bottles and food wrappers strewn on the Formica counters and avocado carpet. Her mom, hair uncombed and wearing only a T-shirt with no bra, looked sullen. She didn't interact with Sophie. She didn't make eye contact. Sophie wracked her tiny brain to figure out what she had done, or what she could do - but of course, she had nothing to do with it.

Through the dark days and the sunny days, time continued to slip into the future. Soon, Sophie was walking and learning to talk. Her vocabulary was limited to the basics, such as the names of familiar objects and action words like eating. There was so much to explore, so much to take in. She learned to color and play with dolls. She discovered building blocks and sandboxes. She even went to the park. The slide was huge, and the swings were mesmerizing. The real surprise, however, was the other children - other people her size, other people like her. She found this discovery to be incredible, since she'd had no idea that other small people existed.

Although nervous and shy, she also had a strong desire to make friends. She hadn't yet learned social norms or how to know whether her friendship was welcome. Sophie, dressed in a motley display of mismatched clothing, ran over and threw her arms around one unsuspecting victim. She held on too tightly for too long. He stood with his arms straight down by his sides and a distressed look on his face.

"I love you," Sophie said as she pressed herself even closer.

"Mom!" he yelled.

His mother looked around to see who was with the girl squeezing her son, at which point Sophie's mom ran over and pulled her off of him with some difficulty.

Undaunted, Sophie ran around squealing and shrieking in delight. There was another little girl with brown hair and a blue dress. She was about the same size as Sophie. They ran up the jungle gym together. They went down the slide one after the other. They were running and jumping and laughing. It was grand.

The day was bright and sunny as if the whole world were joining in to celebrate this moment. The colors were vibrant, the grass a vivid green. Trees were budding with the new leaves of spring. Birds were singing in the trees. Sophie could feel the warmth of the sun on her face. All around her, the earth sang and danced with joy. The background static had been replaced with a symphony of glorious, celestial music. The energy of despair was superseded by an energy of expectancy and wonder. It was so beautiful, she could have cried. The sharp contrast between pain and rapture vied for her devotion and nearly tore her heart in two.

Sophie had started to blame herself for the dark times but she did not give herself credit for the lighter times. She had internalized her mother's sadness and depression and taken it on as her own. Her innocence had been replaced by guilt. She loved this park, and the girl in the blue dress, but she wasn't sure if she deserved to be here. *What if that girl finds out there's something wrong with us?*

Somewhere deep inside, in the unseen and unspoken parts of Sophie's mind and heart was the faint echo of a memory - the memory of a world where she remained forever innocent and pure, a world where life was happy and beautiful, a world where she belonged. She felt a longing for what her soul remembered, but that her mind could not grasp. It was like a ghost, haunting and teasing her from the shadows of her conscious awareness, just present enough to make her heart ache for what she could never have.

Just beyond the grasp of her sensory perception lay the world of Oneness and perfection. What her eyes could not see and her ears could not hear was countless beings of light beings supporting her and wanting to convey to her just how loved and lovable she was. They understood that her feelings of inadequacy and self-doubt were nothing more than her perception - a perception based on the limitations of her five senses, a perception dependent on the actions and attitudes of the people in her life, a perception distorted by the corrupt reality in which she found herself.

Sophie couldn't perceive or touch these ethereal beings. She couldn't access their unconditional love and support. Her experience of love was, by contrast, very conditional, subject to the whims and moods of her parents, a commodity to be bartered in exchange for pieces of her essence. Her happiness and self-expression were contingent on the approval of others.

While this other world of love and beauty surrounded her, it remained just out of sight. The distorted reality, on the other hand, overwhelmed her senses and saturated her awareness. The experience of want and lack was compelling. It felt unshakably real. Sophie was starting to become convinced that it was the only reality there was.

Chapter 2

The Split

The fighting was getting worse. Sophie's parents, Justine and Caleb, were suffering under the strain of life's demands, not the least of which was taking care of a young child. In many ways, they were still children themselves, emotionally unequipped to deal with the conflict of married life or the challenges of being a grown-up. The stress of bills, keeping up with a household, and taking care of a toddler 24/7 was taking a toll. Justine's drinking wasn't helping.

Sophie was woken up by a loud crash from somewhere outside her room. She felt terror and panic wash over her, and she began to cry.

"Great, now you woke up the baby!" She heard her dad yell. The screaming back and forth continued for a while. "I'm leaving!" he shouted as he slammed the front door.

Then it was quiet - too quiet. She wondered if anyone was there. Was she all alone in the house? She kept crying, hoping someone, anyone would come to let her know she wasn't completely abandoned, that she hadn't been left here to die all alone. *Is my mom okay? Where is Dad going? Is he coming back?* A million questions that she couldn't put words to swirled in her toddler mind. *What were they arguing about? Is it my fault?*

Finally, after an unbearable amount of time, her mom came into the room. She had been crying too and was slumped over as though defeated.

"It's okay, Sophie," her mom said in a voice she had already come to recognize as intoxicated. "It's okay," she repeated.

Sophie's mom gave her a sippy cup and put her back in the crib. But Sophie didn't want to be left in the crib. She needed someone to hold her and reassure her that everything was going to be okay, but her mom didn't have the energy for that. She was hanging on by a thread, and a crying baby was simply more than her nerves could stand. Juice, rather than attention, was what she offered Sophie, a sweet distraction to shut her up.

Relieved that someone was still in the house, Sophie felt her panic go down a notch or two. It wasn't gone, but it went down a little. She held the juice cup and accepted the comfort it offered. Her crying stopped.

"There, there," her mom said as she stumbled out of the room.

Sophie's room seemed especially dark that night. It felt big and empty and lonely. When the cup was empty, she intuitively knew not to cry. Her dad had yelled at her mom for waking the baby right before he left. She was figuring out that crying or speaking up might be dangerous. She decided that she had best keep quiet, or something bad might happen. She lay in crib, wondering if her dad would ever come home. *If only I hadn't started crying.*

When her mom got Sophie up the next morning, her dad was not there. Her mom was quieter and more somber than usual. She went through the motions of getting Sophie's breakfast, cleaning her up, and getting her dressed. She was there, but she wasn't there. Sophie tried to smile and be adorable to cheer her up, but she couldn't get a reaction. Her mom looked right through her as if she were invisible. Silence echoed throughout the entire house.

Sophie played with her toys and watched TV, but mostly she tried to keep quiet and stay out of the way. She wondered when her dad would come home. She wondered if he would come home. Her survival instinct began to go into overdrive. It seemed she had already lost one caretaker so she needed to make sure the remaining one was okay. Mom didn't look or act okay. She was barely there, shuffling rather than walking, staring blankly at the table or the wall or the door.

Even though Sophie was still a small child, she sensed that she had more resilience and resourcefulness than her mother. Her inner light had not yet been snuffed out. She believed she could lend a little of her light to her mom to revitalize her. It was almost as if when Sophie was around her, she could see her mom glowing a little brighter, and feel herself glowing a little dimmer. By giving her caretaker some of her life force, she could ensure her physical survival and well-being. She made it her job to make sure her mom was okay, thereby ensuring that she was okay.

Behind the scenes, her guides and angels wept with grief that at such a tender age, Sophie had entered into this deal with the devil, this insidious compromise to dim her light in exchange for safety and love.

"Shine your light bright, Sophie!" they urged. "You are loved unconditionally. You are supported limitlessly. We see you!"

She could not see them nor hear them, but in some very far-off way, she felt them. However, she misinterpreted that warm feeling as confirmation that she was on the right track - that rescuing her mom from despair and self-destruction was moving herself in the right direction to be loved and safe and worthy. She might not be worthy of love as she was right now, but she would prove her worth by taking care of her mom and making her happy. She unconsciously took on the noble role of caretaker.

Sophie soon learned that quiet, obedient and caring children got a lot of praise and attention from adults. "She's such a nice girl," she would hear one say, or "She's so well behaved." Her little ears would perk up at times like these. She seemed to have stumbled upon a surefire strategy for gaining positive attention and approval. Somewhere inside of her, she made a decision. She would be the good girl, a people pleaser.

Sophie wasn't consciously aware of any of these decisions. They were being formed at the foundational level of her operating system and would later come to be known as her personality. An ego identity was being created, a way to get along in life, a way to be safe and accepted. This persona wasn't the truth of who she was or the limit of what she was. In her essence, she was a limitless, divine being. However, in order to navigate this limited, not-so-divine world, she needed to create a pragmatic and workable identity - one that would allow others to label her and place her in a neat little box with well-defined borders.

Sophie worked hard to make her mom happy but no matter what she did, she could not compete with her mother's whiskey or the string of men who frequented the house at all hours of the day and night. Justine, desperate to fill the empty hole inside her own heart, gave far more attention to these men than she did her own daughter. She reduced herself to an emotional parasite, feeding where she could, with nothing left to give.

Every time her mother would bring home a new man, she would seem so happy. She was all laughter and smiles and hugs and kisses. This made Sophie feel left out and disturbed in a stomach-churning way. She would, however, feel a small sense of relief that the burden of her mom's happiness and well-being was lifted from her for a moment. When her mom was without a man, Sophie felt the full weight of her mother's despair on her own young shoulders. As uncomfortable as it was having another one of her mother's lovers invade her space, she would always hope that this time things would work out, that this time she would have an ally to support her in taking care of her mother.

But invariably, the relationship would deteriorate into some version of chaos, with yelling, crying, threats, doors slamming, and her mother winding up once again all alone with her daughter. She would drink and cry and cling to Sophie for comfort.

"At least I have you. You'll never leave me, will you, Sophie?" she sobbed.

Sophie felt a mixture of revulsion at her mother's pathetic demeanor, and elation at being seen and wanted for the first time in weeks.

"I love you, Mommy. I'll never leave you," she promised with all the earnestness of her four-year-old heart.

During each romantic escapade, Sophie was an afterthought. She felt ignored and insignificant. In contrast, the affection and attention she received after a breakup felt like a euphoric high. The cycle of withdrawal and reconnection created an intensity of craving and satisfaction that had an addictive quality to it. The pain was so great, but the resolution so indescribably delicious. It almost felt worth it.

It was during the off times, when her mother was deeply entangled with a man, when Sophie was brushed aside to entertain and take care of herself, that she would enter a world of her imagination that held her spellbound. She created a fantasy world where she was a princess, and everyone was happy all the time, and everybody loved one another, and everything was beautiful and perfect. When she was fully immersed in her imaginary world, it felt more real than the one where people fought and drank and got sad.

She would imagine being held by a beautiful angel and smile a beautiful, restful smile. All the light beings around her smiled too.

Chapter 3

The Kinder Years

Sophie had all but forgotten the other world that called to her in moments of quiet reverie. She was solidly in this world now and coming to know it as the completeness of reality.

Most days, her mom would drop her off on her way to work. Day care had been scary at first, but as she progressed to preschool and kindergarten, it became a part of her normal routine. Days were organized into various activities: the ABC's, counting, coloring, and playtime. Sophie always received accolades from her teachers when she helped clean up and put toys away. That felt really good.

Sophie was exceptionally bright. In addition to basic academic skills, she was learning social skills. In particular, she was learning how to get along and be liked. At home, she often felt like she was in the way or a nuisance. She found it difficult to anticipate her mother's reactions on any given day. The slightest infraction could cause her mother's anger to rain down upon her. There were times, of course, when she did feel like she was good and acceptable and truly wanted, but she could never sustain her mother's approval. She remembered one time when she had helped with the dishes. Her mom was so pleased and kept complimenting her on how sweet she was and how well she was doing. But then Sophie had broken one of the dishes.

"Imbecile! You always mess everything up!" her mother had screamed.

Those words did something to her. Something inside of Sophie was beginning to break.

In kindergarten, however, Sophie's strategy of being the teacher's helper worked swimmingly. It made her feel important and needed. She would have traded being loved for being needed in an instant, but being needed was a pretty secure place to be. She decided that being needed was at least better than being alone.

These decisions were made in the deepest parts of her soul, unspoken agreements made well outside of her conscious awareness. She made all sorts of agreements, at a time when she was so young that she would never remember, stored in places that would be almost impossible to find, fused with her neurology in ways that would make it terrifying to question.

Every day, Sophie participated in all the daily activities. She played when it was time to play. She learned when it was time to learn. She was quiet when it was time to be quiet.

Around Mother's Day, during arts and crafts, the teacher, Ms. Tiffany, told the kids they were going to make Mother's Day cards. Sophie was happy that she could make a gift to give to her mom. More than anything, she wanted to make her mother happy. The teacher showed them how the letter M turned into a W when you turned it upside down. She instructed them to write the word MOM upside down.

As the teacher walked around, checking on all of their work, she stopped at Sophie's table. "What's this?" She asked Sophie.

"It's Mom upside down," she told her.

Puzzled, Ms. Tiffany looked at Sophie's picture of a stick figure doing a handstand. It took several seconds for the penny to drop.

"Oh!" she exclaimed, stifling a laugh. "Very nice, Sophie. I'm sure your mom is going to love it," she encouraged her.

Sophie's heart swelled with pride. She couldn't wait to give it to her mom.

Celeste was Sophie's best friend. They were two peas in a pod and always hung out together on the playground. Sophie could feel that Celeste genuinely liked her. It was wonderful and made her feel happier than she had ever felt around anyone. They held hands and sang songs and always sat next to each other. *This must be what it's like to have a sister.* In a world where people and situations were full of little compromises, Celeste was her one constant, the one person she could count on to always like her and want her just as she was. Celeste didn't even need her for anything. She chose Sophie for Sophie. It felt real.

In that part of her that was even deeper than the hidden part, she felt a trace of remembering. She had felt this real kind of love before - the kind that didn't have to be earned. There was no reference for it. It was just a feeling, or rather, a knowing. As she leaned ever so slightly into that unknown place that she could neither grasp nor see, her guides and angels rushed all around her, hugging her.

"Sophie, we're right here! We love you. Remember who you are, Sophie. You are so brave and so powerful. We are so proud of you!"

But she could not hear them. Merging realities separated once again, and the moment was gone.

"Sophie! I love you, Sophie," Celeste said, waving wildly. "Bye, I'll miss you, Sophie!"

"I love you too." Sophie waved back.

She thought Celeste was just saying goodbye for the day. She did not realize that Celeste was saying goodbye forever.

The next day, Sophie arrived at school, happy and eager as always to see her best friend, Celeste. Looking around in confusion, she asked the teacher where she was.

"They moved, honey. She's not coming back."

Sophie didn't understand. Like a dog that sits interminably by the door, awaiting his master's return, she waited for Celeste to come back. She didn't understand what "moving" meant. She didn't understand the unthinkable truth: that Celeste was never coming back, ever. For days she waited, a little sad, a little anxious, but ever hopeful. But as days turned into weeks, hope was replaced with resignation that the one best thing she had known in her short life was gone. Her little heart was broken.

Sophie continued to play when it was time to play and learn when it was time to learn and be quiet when it was time to be quiet and do what she was supposed to do. She continued to learn social skills and how to get along. But she learned something else too. She had learned, twice now, that if people loved you, they might leave. She had learned that unconditional love was too good to be true, too good to last. She was building a wall around her heart to keep hurt out, not knowing that that same wall would keep love out too.

She added this piece of evidence to her not-yet-fully formed idea that it was safer to be needed than to be loved. Her fledgling belief was beginning to solidify. *Be nice and make yourself useful. Got it.*

Chapter 4

Another Time and Place

The marketplace was bustling this morning. The air was alive with people talking, laughing, and yelling to one other. Merchants were peddling their wares. Buyers examined their offerings and haggled for the best price. Madeleine drank it all in—the excited voices, the display of goods from fruit to chickens to freshly baked bread, the smiles, the looks of skepticism, the women in their frocks, the men in their peasant shirts. She stopped to admire a bunch of flowers, vibrant with color. It was all so glorious.

Madeleine loved these mornings when she was tasked with going to buy the ingredients for the day's menu. She was always careful not to let her face show any enthusiasm for her assignment, lest she be punished for indulging in any simple pleasure and the job be reassigned to someone else. Looking as somber as possible, she had gathered the baskets and jugs required to collect the necessary items.

Once at the market, she was free—free to smile, free to feel. She stood there, feeling the warmth of the sun on her face. A wave of relief washed over her. She took a deep, deep breath of fresh air. Here at the market, she could almost be anyone. She could be a woman buying food for her own family. She could be a fair maiden, happy with the expectancy of meeting a suitor. She could just be. In that brief moment, it felt safe to remember happier times.

Her mind wandered to memories of her mother, who had brought her here to this very market so many times. An image of the two of them sitting in a meadow, with wildflowers all around, came into her mind. They were laughing and singing. Her mom placed a flower in Madeleine's hair and told her how beautiful she was. As she gazed at the flowers at a vendor's table, a little smile flashed across her face. She remembered what it felt like to be happy.

Those times were gone now. Both her parents had died of influenza what seemed like a lifetime ago. She had watched with bewilderment as one after the other—her father first, then her mother—succumbed to what had started as a benign illness. It was a completely unnecessary death.

She had only been nine years old when it happened. Her mother had tried to shield her from the gruesome details of her father's downward spiral, but when her mom got sick herself, there was no one else to care for her but Madeleine. She saw it all. The coughing had turned into air hunger, and her mother gasped for breath as fluid filled up her lungs. Her skin was pale and clammy, eyes sunken in. Eventually, the labor of breathing became shallow and ineffectual. Madeleine was there when her mother took her last breath.

A mix of stark terror, grief, and confusion came over her body. She ran to the neighbor's house, sobbing, "She's dead, she's dead!"

The neighbor shooed her away. "Get away from me! You'll be the death of all of us!"

"That girl is cursed," she heard another say.

Eventually, they came to take her mother's body away, lifeless and cold. That image was burned into her brain, and nothing could ever make it go away. For years, she would wake up in the night, reliving the horror of what she had seen. She wondered what kind of god would create a world like this.

She was all alone now, an orphan. No fate more dire could fall upon a young girl. She was thrust into a harsh reality without warning, all alone, destitute, and hungry. Driven by this hunger and survival instinct, she found herself willing to do whatever she could in exchange for any morsel of food. She quickly learned that charity and goodwill, pontificated by the church and prominent members of society, were empty words. Their true moral code was to exact justice rather than extend mercy.

She was treated as if her circumstances were the result of her own wrong-doing, the judgment of a harsh yet righteous god. She was told that the clergy helping her would be to coddle the weak, to intervene in God's justice and prevent her from learning the lessons her soul needed to be saved from the eternal flames of hell. As self-appointed servants of God, they considered themselves the executor of God's will. They justified their withholding and cruelty, claiming it was for her own good.

Rather than them caring for her as a child who had already suffered the insufferable, she was to be taken on as an indentured servant. They would see to it that she, a lowly street rat, would be offered food and shelter in exchange for laboring in the home of one of the members of the council. They reminded her that their charity was more than she deserved. Her new master reiterated frequently that it was only because of his generosity and goodwill that he could even tolerate her existence. God's servants polished their halos as she scrubbed his floors.

As she stood here, on this day, in the marketplace, life expressing itself all around her, she allowed herself to imagine what things might be like if there were a loving god that would intervene on her behalf. A flicker of hope came to life in her wounded heart. Somewhere inside of her, she still knew there was goodness—if not in this world, then somewhere. Surely, these flowers and smiling people were proof of that. With another thirsty gulp, she drank it all in. *Whatever and wherever you are, thank you.*

She would have stood there for the rest of her life, if it were possible, but she could not. Her master would be expecting her home soon. To be more precise, it was the head housekeeper, Hilda, that would be expecting her.

It seemed that the only small pleasure this woman found in her downtrodden, miserable life was getting Madeleine in trouble and watching her suffer. Hilda, an indentured servant for many years, had never known the freedom to create a life of her own. She had never tasted joy or beauty. As an act of misguided revenge, she wielded what little power she had over Madeleine. She was the definition of a petty tyrant.

Madeleine returned from her reverie back to reality. She knew she needed to make up for lost time. She went about filling her basket with the items on the mental list she had taken from Hilda. She had recited the list over and over on her way to the market. *Don't forget anything.* She bought onions and celery and parsley and potatoes. Her basket was heavy and cumbersome by the time she was done, but that was no excuse to be late. She hurried as fast as she could along the footpath back to her master's house.

Judging by the position of the sun, she could tell she had enjoyed her mental vacation a little too long.

"Where have you been?!" Hilda bellowed.

Until that moment, it had never occurred to Madeleine just how much Hilda looked like a cow. Her figure was all rounded belly with spindly legs and her propensity for snacking lent itself to constant chewing.

Snapping herself back from her vision of a mooing bovine with pendulous teats, Madeleine managed to subdue a smirk and responded appropriately. "Getting the vegetables like you asked, ma'am."

"It don't take no half a day to do the shopping," Hilda chided. "You know, I have to let Master Wilson know about this. It would be wrong to let such an infraction go unreported. I can't have a sin like that on my conscience," she added self-righteously.

There would be another beating that night, but not before Madeleine had completed the rest of her chores. She could tell that Hilda took particular delight in knowing she would have the rest of the day to dread the pain that would be inflicted on her delicate, frail frame.

Madeleine started to protest, but before she gave utterance to her plea for mercy, she stopped herself. She knew all too well that begging and pleading only fueled Hilda's sadistic nature, and she refused to give her the satisfaction. To see Hilda's sarcastic smile while she whimpered only rubbed salt in the wound. It hurt far more to express her pain and have it used against her than it did to keep silent. So, Madeleine made a decision. She would push down her tears and sadness and hurt. She wouldn't show it, ever. In time, she wouldn't even feel it.

Chapter 5

Misfit

Sophie awakened as if from a dream. A few images hung in her conscious awareness, strange images of a girl not much younger than herself. She could see her in an old-fashioned dress and with some sort of a covering on her head. She tried to remember the other parts of the dream, but as dreams do, it faded quickly into the mist of timelessness.

Today was the school pizza and pajama party. She had been looking forward to this for weeks. It marked the beginning of Christmas break. She couldn't wait to show everyone her new pajamas and slippers. Her mom had really come through this time. She wasn't going to be embarrassed or hope to be invisible like those other times. She pictured herself talking with the other girls and one of them complimenting her on her outfit. She had always wanted to be cool like the popular girls. Getting dressed, she stopped to admire herself in the mirror, oblivious that her pajamas were a size too small. *Yes!*

She hurried downstairs. Justine, as usual, was passed out on the couch. Sophie had become accustomed to getting herself ready for school. Turning the TV on to watch cartoons while she ate breakfast, she grabbed a bowl of cereal. The milk carton was empty. She would eat it dry. It was easier to pick out the marshmallows anyway, especially without an adult on duty to reprimand her. She glanced at the clock every few minutes. She knew she needed to leave by 7:25 to make it to the bus stop on time.

At 7:23, she put on her coat and grabbed her backpack. She half walked, half ran to the bus stop. It was a cold December day—one of those days when she could see her breath. Sometimes she liked to pretend she was smoking but today she was too focused on showing off her penguin pajamas and bunny slippers.

She saw Sarah first and waved excitedly. "Hi, Sarah!" Sophie exclaimed a little too loudly.

"Oh, hey, Sophie" Sarah replied quietly, hoping no one else would hear their exchange.

"Do you like my new pajamas?" Sophie continued excitedly.

Sarah pretended not to hear her and turned to talk to someone else. The other girls casually formed a circle with Sophie clearly on the outside. She overheard one of them say, "She's so weird."

Sophie felt like she had just had the wind knocked out of her. The blood drained out of her face, and she stood there feeling hollow and empty. It was as if she had just stepped behind a thick glass wall. Everyone's voices sounded very quiet and far away. All she could hear was a loud buzzing sound in her head.

Like Sarah, she pretended not to hear. She had pinned so much hope on the idea that if she looked more acceptable, she would finally be accepted— that with her new pajamas and slippers, she would finally make the cut and be included. It hadn't worked.

The buzzing slowly faded, and she could hear the girls talking and laughing. She imagined that they were laughing at her. *Why do they hate me?* She answered her own question: Because *I'm hideous and stupid.* She had heard this often enough from her mother when Justine was drunk. Maybe it wasn't just the rantings of an alcoholic. Maybe it was true. This was proof of what she had suspected and feared for a long time—proof that she wasn't good enough.

Sophie fought back the tears that began to well up. She had cried that one time in second grade. There had been no empathy or kindness forthcoming. She had been called Crybaby for months. The ramifications of showing that kind of vulnerability were far too dangerous. She would not cry.

The bus arrived. Sophie dejectedly climbed onto the bus and found a seat by herself near the back. Acutely aware of how cold it was, she pulled her coat around her and stared at the floor. She could hear the other kids talking and laughing and tried to shrink down behind the back of the seat in front of her. She wished, as she had so many times, that she could be invisible.

I wish I was dead.

When they arrived at the school, Sophie was the last one to get off the bus. She wanted to make sure the other girls had time to get far away. Watching the other kids running around, playing hopscotch or sharing collector cards, she wondered why she was different. It hadn't always been this way. When she was little, she had run around and had fun like everyone else, but not anymore. Surrounded by dozens of people, she felt starkly alone. *I don't belong.*

The school bell rang and the kids lined up to go into their classrooms.

"Hey, I like your pajamas, Sophie," said a chubby boy with thick glasses. "You look like a whale."

"I'm a penguin" Sophie corrected him, annoyed. *Do I really look like a whale?*

An hour ago, she would have appreciated his compliment and relished the attention. The girls at the bus stop had taken that from her. Her waning confidence and enthusiasm had died another little death.

Sophie walked into the classroom and sat at her desk. The promise of the day's festivities now seemed lackluster. This was like any other day. School had become a test of endurance. Her primary goal was to remain unnoticed. She accomplished this by not standing out in any way—answer when called upon, but remain quiet otherwise; be smart, but not a nerd; be friendly, but not annoying; be nice, but not the teacher's pet. She pretended to be happy when the occasion called for it. She pretended to laugh when something was funny. She pretended to be sad when something was somber. She pretended to be enthusiastic even when something didn't interest her. She had learned to be exactly what people thought she should be, blending into the background unnoticed. Mostly, she pretended things were fine, even though they weren't most of the time. No one would suspect that she was a distressed or troubled child. She certainly didn't need that kind of attention.

Sophie had perfected the skill of pretending at home. Living with an alcoholic, she never knew who she would be waking up to or who would be walking through the door. Always the consummate actress, she seamlessly matched her mood to that of her mother. She suspected that other, luckier girls weren't straddled with the responsibility of taking care of their parents or coddling their emotions. Sophie had learned that her very survival depended on it. She walked on eggshells, always on guard, ever fearful of her mother's outbursts and abuse. Living in an environment that was never safe, her nervous system remained in a constant state of hyper-vigilance.

There were good times, of course. On the days when her mother was sober, they would bake cookies or ride bikes. There were birthday parties and movie nights and lots and lots of normal, fun, happy times. Sophie loved her mother. She really loved her. It was that other person that showed up when she was drinking that she couldn't stand. This other woman was always there, haunting her from the shadows even on the bright days.

Life would be stable for a while, and the walls around Sophie's heart would begin to lower, just a little. She would cautiously try to trust that everything was going to be all right after all. Then she would wake up one morning or come home from school one afternoon, and Mrs. Hyde would be waiting for her with a sneer on her face.

She felt sick to her stomach. *I hate you so much.* She thought it, but she dared not say it. She dared not take one step out of place. She dared not breathe too loudly. Anything and nothing was reason enough for her mother to unload her ire and vehemence on Sophie. It was during these times that her mother would say those awful things that she couldn't get out of her head. Sophie hoped and prayed that what she said wasn't true, but a part of her was already convinced that it was. *I'm worthless and unlovable.*

School had its challenges, but at least it was a reprieve from the chaos at home. The rules were predictable, so as long as she followed them, she was safe. For the most part, she was able to ignore the fact that the other girls never wanted to play with her. She ate alone and played alone, but she always managed to find something interesting to focus on or a good book to get lost in. It wasn't so bad. Even so, she did still wish the other girls would invite her to join them. Whenever she let herself really think about it, she still felt a yearning to be included, even though she usually managed to push those thoughts away or find another distraction.

Today was different because she couldn't not think about it. She had let herself imagine wearing her awesome pajamas and being cool and wanted and a part of the gang. She felt embarrassed and ashamed and exposed. *I should have stayed invisible. I'm so stupid.* Being popular was not for girls like her.

Her mind wandered to Celeste. She could barely remember what she looked or sounded like anymore. What she did remember was what she *felt* like. She missed her. She missed feeling like someone wanted her around, someone who liked her for no reason, which was the best reason. She was reminded that there was some goodness in this world. There was too little of it, but at least there was some. *Thank you, Celeste.*

"Sophie!" he teacher called again.

Sophie looked up to see all the other kids lined up to start the activities that Ms. Somers, Sophie's fourth grade teacher, had planned for the day.

"Are you ready to have fun?" she asked in a peppy voice. Sophie took a deep breath and tucked her emotions away. "Yes, Ms. Somers," she replied with all the enthusiasm she could muster.

The games began with Simon Says. Next came musical chairs, charades, and bingo. Sophie played right along with everyone else. She laughed and jumped and yelled out when she got bingo. There were plenty of snacks and pizza and even soda. Ms. Somers had gone to a lot of effort to make sure their last day before the break was a memorable one. Sophie knew in her head that it was all wonderful; it just didn't feel wonderful. The shadow that pervaded her home life was following her to school.

She gave Ms. Somers a winning smile and a warm hug as she said, "Thank you, merry Christmas!"

"Merry Christmas to you, Sophie," Ms. Somers replied.

Sophie got back on the bus for the return trip home. All the other kids seemed genuinely excited to be off for Christmas break. She imagined they had vacations and parties planned. She imagined they would have lots of presents under their Christmas trees. She imagined they had doting grandparents that would be visiting them for the holidays. *They have good reason to be excited.*

She wondered if her mom would put up any decorations this year. Last year, Christmas had come and gone without much fanfare. There were a couple of presents, but her mom was drunk as usual and didn't feel up to cooking Christmas dinner.

"You don't mind, do you Sophie?" she had asked. "We'll go to McDonald's. You love McDonald's".

Sophie said she didn't mind and pretended to be excited about McDonald's on Christmas. She told herself it wasn't so bad. She was getting good at normalizing the abnormal.

Chapter 6 –

Sinners in the Hands of an Angry God

Sophie sat in Sunday school, listening to the teacher talk about Jesus and a lost lamb. The stories she heard in this room had a very different tone than the sermons the pastor gave from the pulpit. In here, Jesus seemed loving and kind, like a big brother or a best friend. In the main church, God seemed like more of a stern and scary ogre.

Her Sunday school teacher, Ms. Sally, was always soft-spoken and kind. She seemed to have a soft spot for Sophie and would always make sure to give her extra cookies or lemonade. Too young to suspect that her teacher pitied her, Sophie lapped up the attention like a love-starved dog. Her sporadic visits were a small reprieve from her world of vacant adults. Ms. Sally had a way of making her feel cared for, like she mattered.

Sophie's grandparents considered it their duty to make sure she attended church ,where she could learn proper morals. Unlike sweet and gentle Ms. Sally, they reminded her more of the grim preacher, often using terms like "responsibility" and "the right thing to do." They had a way of making her feel uncared for, like she was a burden.

Introducing her to other members of the congregation was a big to-do. It felt like they were putting her on display, as if announcing a charitable donation. They always seemed more interested in talking about her than talking to her. Sometimes, one of the other church members would ask,

"And how's your daughter? We're keeping her in our prayers," side-glancing at Sophie. It felt uncomfortable for reasons she could not explain.

Justine's parents, Barbara and Carl, had been equally stern with their daughter when she was growing up. Nothing she did was ever quite good enough. If she brought home all A's with the exception of one C on her report card, no acknowledgement was given to what she did right. They only and always fixated on her shortcomings. When she cleaned her room, they pointed out the one corner that wasn't spotless. She was clumsy in dance class. She was chubbier than the other girls. They didn't yell or scream or call her names; their abuse was more covert than that. They withheld their love and approval, and they made sure she always knew that she was a disappointment.

Justine's torment was one of inexpressible loneliness, like she was sentenced to live behind a glass wall where no one could see her or hear her. She could not verbalize or even fully comprehend her own pain, because there was nothing tangible to point to. It wasn't about what they did, but about what they didn't do. They withheld encouragement, they withheld affection, they withheld acceptance and approval. It was like living with automatons; they were present physically, but inaccessible emotionally. She both craved their attention and recoiled from their rejection. The unspoken message was clear: she was unlovable.

Over time, Justine gave up on seeking her parents' love and acceptance. She still needed it desperately, but the agony of it always being denied drove her to the brink of insanity. There was nothing she could do to win their favor. From the outside, they seemed like the perfect parents. They were well-to-do, made sure she attended the best schools, provided piano and dance lessons, and took her to church three times a week. They were quick to point out how dedicated they were and how hard they tried. Clearly, Justine was the weak link.

Self-loathing began to set in sometime in high school. Her deep-seated feelings of unworthiness were superseded only by her desperate yearning for love. These antagonizing forces wound around themselves, pulling her first in one direction and then another, manifesting in a hideous display of dysfunctional behavior. A deeply wounded part of her, enraged that she couldn't gain her parents' approval, made sure she would get their attention.

Getting pregnant at seventeen accomplished just that. She had placed them in the proverbial catch-22. They couldn't, as devout Christians, advocate for an abortion, but neither could they condone her promiscuity. So, predictably, they supported her financially, but withheld their blessing. Justine had, unwittingly, perpetuated the cycle. She was a young, uneducated girl having a baby out of wedlock. This act of self-sabotage almost ensured that she would forever remain dependent on her parents to pick up the pieces of her faltering life. It also ensured that she would be forever subject to their criticism.

She hated their stoic perfectionism. She hated the superiority they lorded over her from their ivory tower. Judgement had killed their connection. The two could not exist in the same space.

So, she turned to alcohol both to hide the pain and as a form of self-punishment. It killed two birds with one stone. She could simultaneously punish herself for being defective, and punish her parents for the mistake they had brought into the world. Justine used alcohol to suppress her feelings of unworthiness. She used men to fulfill her longing for love. The two together proved an explosive combination.

In spite of her inability to recognize it, she was a very attractive woman. She had no trouble getting the attention of men, who were all too willing to offer a semblance of love in exchange for sex. It was the perfect deal, each receiving their drug of their choice, feeding their dopamine addiction. It was always great until the crash. Eventually, the high of infatuation would wear off, and inner demons would surface. As they each tried to extort their emotional needs from the other, they oscillated between the roles of victim and perpetrator. Predictably, the relationship would deteriorate into chaos and abuse.

The cycle of the honeymoon phase, jealousy and insecurity, and blaming and fights repeated over and over. Justine had no awareness that she had any responsibility for how or why it was happening. She had worked so hard to bury her pain that it never occurred to her to look within. Facing her trauma, going into the pain to find its origin and pull it out by the root was too terrifying to contemplate. That level of introspection and honesty required more courage than she possessed or was willing to cultivate. It was easier and less threatening to blame the other person and have another drink.

After each debacle, Justine would piece her tattered ego back together as well as she could and turn to the one comfort she could count on: the bottle. It was during these times, in between relationships, that she cried on Sophie's shoulder. She could count on her emotionally neglected daughter to reciprocate her affection. But Sophie's affection was insufficient to satisfy her insatiable need for validation. The emptiness inside of her was like a sucking black hole that could never be filled. Soon enough, another man would enter the scene.

Sophie's grandparents didn't exactly hold it against her that she was an illegitimate child. Nevertheless, she had been conceived in sin and born into sin. They considered it their Christian duty to make sure they took her to church and gave her the opportunity to be absolved. After Sunday school, she would join up with her grandparents and go into the main sanctuary to hear the Good Word.

The service would start with a few hymns. The choir was led by Gladys White, a relic and permanent fixture of God's house. As she had never been married, the church was the only family she knew. Being a servant of God was the whole of her identity, so no one had the heart to tell her what they were all thinking. Week after week, she sang with magnificent gusto—and magnificently out of tune.

Sophie winced and whispered, "They should let somebody else sing."

"Shh!" her grandmother scolded.

Every week, the preacher would rehash the same message with minimal variation. He talked about an all-loving God, and about how Adam and Eve had eaten of the tree of knowledge of good and evil. He talked about how man was born into sin, and that unless a person believed in Jesus Christ as his lord and savior, they would be damned to burn in hell for eternity.

While the preacher droned on, Sophie would doodle in the church bulletin, wiggle her foot back and forth, and stare at the stained-glass windows to see if she could make out pictures with her imagination. She wasn't really listening, but she couldn't help but hear. The theme was morbid and always made Sophie feel depressed. To think that her bleak little life would culminate in eternal suffering was too terrible to bear. *That's just mean.*

Her mind wandered to said bleak little life. She wondered how the world had become the way it was. If she were God, she would never let things be so awful. She knew deep in her soul, that it was never meant to be like this. *What's wrong with this place?*

She felt a wave of guilt move through her to even think such a thought, calling to mind the pastor's rhetoric that "God's ways are higher than our ways, and it's not for man to question." Yet the thought persisted.

She had been taught that God was all-loving, but there was so little evidence of that. It seemed he could either be all-loving or all-powerful but not both. She couldn't sort it all out and wondered if she was the only person who had these kinds of questions. The cautious part of her agreed it was better to play it safe and go along with what they taught her at church. Gambling with eternal damnation was not a risk she was willing to take.

One Sunday, she doodled less and listened more. The preacher spoke once again of sin, but on this day, Sophie tuned in to the message about Jesus and how he loved mankind so much that he had died to save them from the eternal flames of hell. She pictured Jesus as she had seen him in the books in Sunday school. He had one of the kindest faces she had ever seen. Prompted by a combination of fear, guilt, and a longing for love, she answered the altar call and found herself walking down the aisle. She invited Jesus into her heart that day. She felt a warmth she had never felt before, a genuine connection with the divine. The pastor told her that she had been born again. Her experience was real, and it was wonderful.

The trouble came later ,when the church presumed to define her experience by attaching all sorts of rules and doctrines to it. She was told what her experience meant rather than being allowed to decide for herself. Still struggling with the concept of sin and hell, she agonized over the idea of a bipolar god who was all-loving on the one hand, but harsh and punitive on the other. Trying to hold these antithetical ideas in her mind simultaneously resulted in a cognitive dissonance that threatened to fracture her psyche.

The more she was told, the more questions she had. Her heart broke for the innocents born into a world of suffering. *Is it really fair to blame humans for the state of the world?*

Sophie didn't have the answers, but she was asking the right questions, and she would keep on asking, because she couldn't not do so.

Chapter 7

Unwelcome Beauty

Madeleine continued her life of indentured servitude. Little changed from month to month, year to year, except that her body was growing and maturing as dictated by nature. Having no access to a mirror, she did not realize that she was becoming beautiful. Every minute of the day was filled with chores and duties. Her time was occupied with fulfilling every demand placed upon her with exactitude to avoid reprimand or penalty. Her schedule left no room for frivolity, and Hilda had zero tolerance for idleness. She kept her head down and her hands busy.

On occasion, she noticed the master of the house looking at her. He stared unblinkingly, as a predator studies their prey. She had no reference for understanding why his interest in her had changed. She was yet a girl, only thirteen years old. Her dreams still involved playing with dolls, wading in the river, or picking daisies—simple dreams that she had been denied. In her naive and controlled existence, she had had no exposure to boys or men and knew nothing of the ways of the world. She was an innocent.

Hilda had noticed her blossoming— and she hated her for it. She assumed the master's interest would give Madeleine some advantage over her. An older, wiser woman should have had a protective instinct for a young, powerless girl targeted by a sexual predator but Hilda had no such inclinations towards protection or decency. She herself had been sacrificed long ago at the altar of another woman's self-serving ambitions. Ever since compassion and care had long since fled her hardened black heart. She was at once threatened by the attention Madeleine was receiving and eager to see her destroyed by it.

Madeleine had come into womanhood. The day it happened, she was mopping. She saw a spot of blood on the floor, and then another. She traced the origin of the blood and discovered, to her horror, that it was coming from her. She ran to Hilda out of sheer panic. If she had had anyone else in the world, she would have never resorted to seeking Hilda out for any problem. But there was no one else in her desolate life. Hilda was the only option.

"It's the curse," was all Hilda offered, then handed her some rags to handle the situation. "Keep yourself clean, and mind you don't be soiling the floor, or anything else for that matter."

That was it. Madeleine had thought she was dying, bleeding to death. Hilda's lack of concern seemed to indicate that it was normal or to be expected. Madeleine tried to read between the lines, searching for a clue as to how she was to react. Sensing apathy from Hilda, she took her cue to normalize the occurrence. However, that didn't mean she wasn't alarmed; she was very alarmed. *Why am I bleeding? Why was Hilda so indifferent about the situation? Is it ever going to stop? Does this happen to all women?*

Madeleine had no parent figure, no confidante with whom she could entrust her fears. These new and unfamiliar questions were like a gap in her brain with no answers to fill it. Life had already presented her with so many questions that were unanswerable—questions that even the wisest philosophers would have trouble answering, like why had her parents died, and where had they gone? And there was one question that haunted her most: *Is it my fault?*

Hilda had said something that sounded important: "It's the curse." Those words rang in Madeleine's mind. They felt like the truest words she had ever heard. *Cursed—yes, that's it.*

Oddly, hearing that was strangely comforting, not because she wanted to be cursed, but because at last it all made sense. *I'm cursed. That must be it.* She felt a weird sense of relief. She finally had the answer to the question of why. She could stop trying to figure it all out, like some unsolvable riddle set to drive her mad. She could, at last, make peace with her fate and stop struggling to right the wrong. It felt kind of like surrender.

Madeleine lost herself a little more that day. Apathy, laced with resignation, became her baseline reality. It made going through the motions of life easier. It took a lot of energy to maintain hope in a situation that seemed utterly hopeless. Giving up was easier.

Of course, she could never truly give up. Though covered over with layer upon layer of trauma and pain, her divine spark burned eternal.

Life was not done trying to extract every dram of life force energy from Madeleine. She had made peace, so to speak, with the hell of her existence, but she did not know what darkness lay in wait, an unspeakable brutality of which her mind could not conceive, until it happened.

She was chopping vegetables in preparation for the evening meal. There was nothing unusual about this day. Hilda had figured out that Madeleine enjoyed going to the market. While it took a toll on Hilda's beaten-down and worn-out body to make the trek herself, she would be damned if she would allow Madeleine any reprieve from her drudgery.

Madeleine had already done the washing for the day, which included all bedsheets, towels, rags, and clothes. All had to be washed by hand and hung to dry early, so as to take advantage of the sunlight. The water was so cold that her hands stung, her fingertips went numb, and her entire body shivered. Hilda always assigned this job to Madeleine, enabling herself to stay inside where it was warm. After the laundry, Madeleine moved on to dishes and floors, dusting and windows.

Hilda fixed the master's meals, always making a little extra for herself. She treated maintaining the protuberance in her mid section like a part time job. "Just a taste," she would say, "to make sure it's befitting of the boss."

Sophie rolled her eyes. *More like twenty tastes, fat cow.* Hilda never, ever gave Madeleine a taste. Her diet was relegated to a bland and unpalatable slop, devoid of nutrition, sufficing only to keep her alive and in working order.

Madeleine lived in a world of her own invention. As her body went through the motions of cleaning and scrubbing and chopping, her mind wandered to far-off places. She thought less of her parents now. She dreamed more of things unseen and unknown. They might hold her body hostage, but they could not contain her mind. That belonged to her. Her imagination called forth images and people she had never been exposed to in her real life. She had no idea where she drew this information. In a way, this world of fantasy felt more real than the life she woke to every day.

As a flight of ideas blew threw her consciousness, one face, one scenario began to become more prevalent than the others. It was a girl of similar age to herself. The settings and props were unlike any she had seen in her own world. It was all so strange, and yet something about this girl felt familiar, as if she knew her. They shared an innocence and a sadness that Madeleine had not encountered in anyone else before. Once, the girl had looked into her eyes as if she were looking into her. Madeleine felt seen for the first time.

Her introspection was interrupted abruptly.

"Come here, girl," she heard him say. "Stand over there in the light."

Startled, Madeleine timidly walked over by the window as instructed. The master had barely ever spoken a word to her before. She, as a servant, had remained always in the background, like a piece of furniture. She felt a shiver run down her spine. She had made it a practice to always keep her head bent and her eyes down, to remain as invisible as possible. Now she was being asked to make herself visible. Although fully dressed, she felt exposed like a solitary goldfish on display in a small glass bowl.

"Stand over there in the light," he had said. She obeyed because to not obey was to invite punishment, swift and sure. She walked into the light and looked down at the floor.

"Lift your head, girl. Look at me."

Once again, she did as instructed. She felt like a piece of produce showcased at the market, to be inspected for quality, blemishes, and overall acceptability.

"Come closer."

Trepidation turned to fear as she slowly inched towards him. She could feel his ill intent like a thick cloud of evil emanating from his core. She felt weak and naked and exposed. But most of all, she felt powerless, paralyzed to resist, afraid to disagree or agree to whatever was to come next.

As he took her by the hand and led her to his bedroom, she felt herself leave her body. She knew she was walking, knew he closed the door, knew she was taking her clothes off, but it was as if she were watching it happen to someone else.

She wanted to cry out, but she was mute. For whom would she call for help? Hilda? Hilda would never have the courage to stand up to the master, to intervene on Madeleine's behalf, to defend a young girl from the unthinkable. No, Hilda would save her own skin, protect her own interests, and despise Madeleine all the more for what had happened to her.

Madeleine watched, dissociated, from outside her body. Many heavenly hosts pressed around her that day, reaching out to comfort her, holding her in the arms of love, proclaiming her innocence. Madeleine neither heard nor saw. She was numb and blank. The depth of aloneness was like an empty pit that had no bottom, the result of total cosmic abandonment.

A wretched, dirty feeling, that only one who has been violated in this most personal way can know, clung to her like the stench of a skunk. Not a thousand baths nor a thousand years could wash away this defilement. It wasn't on her, nor even in her; it had become her.

As she lay in her bed that night, she realized that even the apathy, for which she had sold her hope, was too good for her. Resignation was not enough to satisfy the god of this world, for there were always new levels of hell. The more she struggled, the more ensnared she became. And the more she surrendered to the struggle, in order to attain some small measure of peace, the more diabolical the subterfuge became.

She could no longer escape into herself. Now she hated being in her body as much as she hated being in the world. Her world of imagination was tainted. Dark images now invaded the spaces where fantasies once lived.

She hoped she would never see the girl from her daydreams again. She could not look at her.

Chapter 8

A Bright Spot

Every now and then, seemingly out of the blue, Sophie's dad would pick her up for a week or two. He had moved out of state after he and her mother had split, so these visits were few and far between. She got to talk to him on the phone every couple of weeks, but her mom always monitored their conversations to make sure she didn't reveal anything incriminating.

Her dad wasn't a bad or even a selfish person. If circumstances had been different, Caleb would have stayed with Sophie's mom and been a dependable and good father. He simply hadn't been prepared for the tidal wave that was Justine. Raised by loving, emotionally intelligent parents, he had faced relatively little adversity growing up. His parents had encouraged rather than criticized, were involved rather than distracted, affectionate rather than cold. Caleb was generally happy and well adjusted.

They had fallen in love at seventeen, high school sweethearts. Justine was beautiful, shy, and unsure of herself. Caleb was handsome and outgoing. There was no love like young love. With hearts open and trusting, as yet unscathed by heartbreak or betrayal, they fell madly in love. They got carried away on a river of hormones and emotions. In just a couple of months, Justine turned up pregnant.

Tongue in cheek, Caleb's dad had responded jokingly but firmly, "What do you call a boy who gets a girl pregnant? Daddy."

Caleb had been raised to be both honorable and respectable. There wasn't much to think about. He would do the right thing.

Justine, on the other hand, had been all but disowned by her parents and was subjected to an unending stream of guilt and denigration. Caleb's parents helped the young, expecting couple get a small apartment and set Caleb up with a job working for his dad. The plan was for them to get married after the baby was born, as Justine didn't want to wear a wedding gown that showed her baby bump.

It hadn't taken long for Justine's childhood traumas and maladaptive coping mechanisms to surface. She became reactive to everything Caleb did or didn't do, said or didn't say. He was completely unprepared for the yelling, screaming, and unsolicited accusations. Her insecurity drove her to be jealous of every interaction he had with females, on or off the job. The verbal and at times physical attacks were relentless. She had a stamina for fighting that tore him apart and wore him out. He had never seen nor could ever have imagined living in a hell like this. He dreaded coming home.

After Sophie had been born, things only got worse. Pouring gas on her already raging fire, Justine started drinking regularly. Their fights became explosive. If pulling his hair out would have helped, Caleb would gladly have plucked them one by one. He tried everything. Nothing worked. He was beside himself.

He sought comfort and advice from his parents. They had witnessed enough to know he wasn't exaggerating. It was a difficult and dire situation. There were no simple solutions. All they could offer was to let him know that they supported him in whatever decision he made. Their love was unconditional.

The day Caleb walked out, he knew he wasn't coming back. Justine had taken him to the breaking point. He was wrought with guilt and fear for his baby girl, but he knew beyond a shadow of a doubt that staying was not the solution. He tried to get Sophie on the weekends, but Justine always started another fight, made false accusations, and tried to pull him back into her web. When she finally figured out that her ploys were not going to work, she chose to hurt him the only way she could—by withholding his daughter. His freedom, joy, and even his peace were an affront to her existence. Wracked with pain, Justine felt a compulsion to inflict pain on others.

Caleb's parents had helped him find a lawyer and gone to court with him to fight for partial custody, but the judge hadn't ruled in his favor. Several years and thousands of dollars later, he had let it go, settling for minimal visitation.

Sophie was not privy to any of this information. Instead, she was left with a million questions. Receiving no answers, her wounded psyche filled in the blanks with the worst possible explanations. *He doesn't want me anymore.*

Sophie loved spending time with her dad. It also meant she got to spend time with Nana and Papa Joe. He would pick her up and take her to her grandparents' house a couple of hours away. They had a dog named Ginger and a lazy cat named Viola who was convinced that Sophie's bed was, in fact, hers. Sophie indulged Viola's territorial nature, even allowing her to sleep on her pillow, in exchange for turning her into her fur baby.

"What in the world?" Nana yelled down the hall. Hearing Viola's screeches, she peeked in to see what the ruckus was all about. She found Sophie stuffing the cat into one of her doll dresses.

"We're having a tea party, and she wants to look pretty." Sophie explained.

"It doesn't sound like she wants to," Nana replied.

Viola, with the dress half on and half off and a bonnet pulled down over one of her eyes, looked dismayed and disheveled. Nana intervened on her behalf, negotiating a compromise with Sophie.

"She already has such a beautiful fur coat, Sophie. God made her with her clothes already on. Maybe we should let her show off her natural beauty. What do you think?"

Having already been scratched by the protesting Viola, Sophie conceded. "Alright. You can wear your birthday suit, but you need to mind your manners," she scolded.

Nana always made a big breakfast with eggs and bacon and pancakes. Sophie got to eat in her pajamas and watch TV or play with toys for a couple of hours in the morning. At Nana's, she could relax and ease into her day. Nobody yelled. Nobody drank. Best of all, it just felt normal.

Since her dad so rarely got to see her, he tended to be the proverbial Disneyland dad. They would go for ice cream. He would buy her toys. He took her to theme parks or somewhere special at least once per visit. It was totally amazing, a completely different world. When she was here, she could pretend she was like any other girl, with people who loved her and looked after her. She didn't have to be the responsible one or worry if her mother was going to be okay. For two glorious weeks, she could just be a kid. Her body began to decompress.

Sophie especially loved spending time with Nana. She glowed with love and sweetness unlike anyone Sophie had ever been around. She never saw her without a smile on her face and a twinkle in her eye.

"You look like an angel," Sophie said to her once.

"Oh, child, you are *my* angel." Then, winking, she added, "It takes one to know one."

It felt like her Nana had a secret—a wonderful secret that no one else knew: that life was beautiful.

One afternoon, Sophie and her Nana were baking cookies. Her dad had gone fishing with Papa Joe. It was just the two of them at home. Nana put on some music. They danced in the kitchen and ate cookie dough out of the bowl. While the cookies were cooling, Nana told Sophie stories of her childhood.

She had grown up on a farm in Montana. She only highlighted the pleasant and happy parts of her personal history. Sophie listened with rapt attention as Nana told her about their snowy winters and beautiful horses and her pet cow named Clarabelle. It sounded like a wonderful place to grow up, so very unlike her own childhood. She wished she could have grown up on a farm.

What Nana was careful to omit were the stories of her mentally unstable father, who beat them frequently and fervently. Her mother, Sophie's great-grandmother, never intervened on her daughter Daisy's behalf. Daisy's mother had suffered at the hands of her husband often enough to know that if she stood up to him, he would shift his focus, and she would incur his wrath upon herself. She had neither the courage nor the inclination to protect her children, offering them up instead as sacrificial lambs to appease the monster. She watched silently as he berated them, beat them, and banished them to the psychological torture of solitary confinement. Daisy couldn't decide which she despised the most: the sadistic antics of her schizophrenic father, or the complicit cowardice of her pathetic mother. One thing she knew for sure: she didn't have room in her life for either of them. The day she turned eighteen, she walked out the door and never looked back.

Something in Daisy's soul shone brighter than the rest. Her siblings succumbed to the social conditioning of their circumstances. They gave themselves over to petty jealousies and rivalries, vying to be the fanciest pig in the parlor. Unable to imagine anything beyond their miserable life, they chose between the only options they knew—victim or abuser— thus perpetuating the cycle of dysfunction and generational trauma. Daisy did not yield to this temptation. She was an overcomer. She prevailed through the countless trials and emerged not unscathed, but beautiful and strong. Her brother and sister followed the path of the common man. Daisy took the road less traveled.

Nana always made Sophie feel like she was the most important person in the world. She made the food she liked and watched the shows she liked. They played board games and did puzzles together. She taught her gardening and needlepoint. Nana congratulated her when she got anything right and never criticized when she got it wrong. She made a big deal of Sophie's drawings and always put them on the refrigerator. She was, in a word, wonderful. She was the one thing in Sophie's world that was good and right and as it should be. The time Nana spent with her filled her cup and gave her the oomph to carry on.

It was great spending time with her dad too, but she always felt like there was something between them. Justine, still bitter about the divorce, never hesitated to bad-mouth Caleb. She filled Sophie's head with ideas that her dad didn't really love her, and when she was drunk, she would go so far as to tell Sophie that it was her fault that he had left. Her mother's words stuck in Sophie's subconscious mind like hypnotic suggestions, eroding her self-esteem, undermining her connection with her dad, and reinforcing her belief that she was unlovable. She wanted to ask him outright, "Do you love me?" But she couldn't bring herself to ask, because she was too afraid of the answer.

While it was reassuring to spend time with him, she had trouble trusting him. He acted like he loved her, but how could she know for sure? *People pretend all the time.* After all, she herself had become very adept at pretending. She wished she felt the same way about him that she did about Nana.

With Nana, there was no wondering. She knew her Nana loved her inside and out, and she trusted it. Nana's love was the one thing she could count on.

One afternoon, as Sophie and Daisy were sitting in the kitchen, Sophie looked over at her and said, "I feel like we've always known each other, always and always, even before you were my Nana."

Sophie didn't know where these words had come from, exactly. It was as if a distant memory had surfaced from another time and place, a memory of the two of them together. She was still a little girl, but Nana was younger—not young like her, but younger like her mother.

"Is that so?" Nana responded. "Tell me about it."

"Well, you were my mom, and we would play and dance in the flowers. I love you, Nana, forever and ever."

Daisy didn't question Sophie. She suspected that they had been together before, in many lifetimes, in fact. They had played many roles in each other's lives, sometimes parent and child, other times siblings or friends. Nana's face glowed more than usual in that moment. She looked at Sophie and smiled. Gently taking her granddaughter's hand in hers, she said, "I love you too, Sophie, forever and ever."

Chapter 9

A Sense of Self

Soon Sophie was back home again—back to reality as she knew it. Her mom fawned over her, sloppily hugging and kissing her, telling her how much she'd missed her and that she couldn't bear for her to ever leave her again. Sophie felt the urge to pull away. She didn't, because she knew it would invite a guilt trip or worse. It was easier and safer to allow her mom to cling to her and for Sophie to go along with it. It didn't feel like she was receiving a hug—more like one was being taken from her, like her energy was being syphoned off. Fighting her impulse to pull away, she stiffened and contained her resistance.

As her body got bigger, a greater awareness of herself as a separate being was beginning to evolve. She was growing tired of her identity as an extension of her mother. Though still dependent on her mom for food and shelter, she felt less pressure to be invisible to maintain her own safety.

The fear and worry that had consumed her emotional experience was making room for a new emotion. Resentment was beginning to join the party. Her critical thinking was kicking in, and she was able to compare her situation to that of others. She saw other mothers at school and at the store. She knew everyone wasn't dealing with an alcoholic who was evicted regularly for not paying rent, who spent the grocery money on booze, who had a string of lovers like a revolving door, of whom she was too embarrassed to ever invite a friend over.

Sophie was caught in the middle of two conflicting forces pulling her one way and then the other. Justine was, after all, the only mother she had.

Her love might be toxic, but it was the only love Sophie had. She wished she didn't crave her mother's love and acceptance so much. She wished she didn't fear her mother's rejection so much. She at once despised her and desperately needed her. She felt sick to her stomach.

The afternoon she came home from school to an empty fridge and pantry was the first time she felt the anger boil up almost uncontrollably. She was going through a growth spurt. She felt hungry all the time, largely because she never got enough to truly feel full. Ravenous, she had almost run home from school as visions of fried boloney and cheese toast danced in her head. Rushing through the door, she searched every cupboard and drawer. She found nothing.

It started in her face. She felt hot and flushed. It quickly moved into her scalp and down into her chest. She wanted to scream and stomp about and throw things. For the first time, she understood rage.

Her mother was lying on the couch, passed out as usual. For a split second, the thought of shaking her by the shoulders and yelling at her felt satisfying, but Sophie knew that to indulge this temptation was both absurd and counterproductive. Fighting, accusations, and a pathetic display of blame-shifting would ensue. It would only compound the problem at hand.

Sophie grew up a lot that day. Her mom had clearly demonstrated that she was incapable of providing her with the most basic of needs. She would have to go hungry today, but she was going to figure something out and learn how to take care of herself.

Taking a hard look at her mother with her unkempt hair, dark circles under her eyes, swollen belly, skinny legs, and splotchy skin, she saw a pitiful creature. Alcohol had taken all that was beautiful and good from Justine, leaving her more creature than human.

I'll never let that happen to me.

In so many ways, from the moment of conception, the underpinnings of who she was had been decided for her, precognitively and preverbally. Sharing her mother's DNA and spending nine months in the womb, Justine was in her and *was* her in a way Sophie couldn't consciously comprehend. Later, as a small child, she had taken on her mother's poverty, guilt, and shame as her own. Without realizing it, her self-worth had been inextricably tied to how her mother was perceived.

That day, Sophie began to disentangle her identity from that of her mother. She consciously made a decision and gave herself permission to be a separate and different person. She didn't know, just yet, who she wanted to be. She only knew one thing for sure: she didn't want to be like her mother. Justine was pathetic and weak and dependent on men. Sophie would be independent and strong. Life had taught her that she couldn't rely on anyone, so she resolved to take care of herself and to need no one. Sophie placed herself behind an impenetrable wall of self-protection. *No one will hurt me. No one will let me down.*

Sophie was too smart to run away. That would be reckless and dangerous. Jumping out of the frying pan into the fire of being placed in foster care was far too risky. She would bide her time and find ways to get through the next few years. Babysitting was a way she could earn enough money to ensure she had food with a little left over for clothes. Observing the lives of several adults she knew, she pondered their various professions and the kind of respect they commanded. A game plan was forming. She would rise above her childhood. She would be better than all this.

Sophie was a gifted student. Up until now, her performance had been mostly motivated by pleasing her teachers and winning approval. That was changing. Fueled by ambition, she made a decision: to be a lawyer. She pictured herself walking into court, wearing a suit, briefcase in hand, head held high. Everyone looked at her and spoke to her with respect. It felt good. This was a solid plan.

Sophie began to excel academically. Long gone were the days of mean girls making her cry. She might not be popular, but she no longer cared. She had more important things to worry about. While the popular girls were squandering their time on cheerleading and boys, she was studying, participating in clubs, volunteering, and being active on the student council. She strategically began getting all her ducks in a row. It wasn't enough for her to be a good student. Reliant on getting a scholarship, she would have to go above and beyond, to be a shining star.

Finding time to babysit became even more essential. Justine certainly couldn't be counted on to pay for her extracurricular activities.

On a Saturday evening in September, Sophie showed up for one of her regular babysitting jobs. Mr. Douglas answered the door and ushered her in.

"Hi, Mr. Douglas. Where is Mrs. Douglas?" Sophie queried.

"She and the kids went to her mother's house," he replied.

"Oh," Sophie responded, surprised that they hadn't phoned her to let her know. They were usually good at communicating if there were any changes.

"Have a seat, Sophie. Can I get you something to drink?" Mr. Douglas went on. His behavior was uncustomary, and he sounded nervous.

Sophie felt a strange sensation go up her spine. Something about this scene felt familiar—not intimately, but in a far-off way. For all of the strange and unwelcome men her mother had invited into their home, Sophie had escaped injury. By the grace of God or the angels or the great unknown, she had attracted neither their attention nor ill intention. She had never herself been in this situation before, yet it felt reminiscent of an incident both personal and threatening.

Sophie sat stiffly on the couch. "No, thank you," she replied to his offer of a drink.

"Tell me, Sophie, what are your plans for your future? Are you going to university? I'm only asking because I wondered if you might need my help in any way. A girl like you could benefit greatly from a benefactor. We've always appreciated how conscientious and hardworking you are. I appreciate you, Sophie."

The last statement was made with a different tone and inflection.

"Thank you, sir," Sophie responded modestly.

"You know, you really are quite beautiful." He went on. Mr. Douglas sat next to her and touched her cheek with his fingertips, lifting her face up and towards him as if he intended to kiss her.

He stared at her. She looked down. She didn't have a conscious reference for what was about to happen, but somewhere, in her intuition, she knew. If this situation had occurred even six months prior, she would have silently submitted and gone along with the adult in the room. She would have fallen prey to one of millions of men who targeted young innocents who were still conditioned to obey and had not yet found their voice.

But Sophie was no longer naive. Understanding her mother's weakness had made her strong. She recognized that adults were not always the most powerful or virtuous, and children did not always have to defer to their lead.

A rage, stronger than fear, began to kindle inside of her as she envisioned herself standing up and punching him right in the face. She sat for one of those eternal moments as time stood still, not thinking, but tuning into something beyond what her eyes and ears could see and hear.

An almost audible voice thundered inside her head, "*Run!*" She didn't know where the voice came from. It sounded like a clear, distinct single voice and a thousand voices all at once. She felt herself leap up like a springbok antelope, her legs running full-out towards the door. She did not concern herself with politeness or goodbyes. She didn't stop running until she was all the way back to her house.

As she lay in bed, her heart still racing, Sophie wanted to tell someone, but she didn't know who to tell. Her mother, she felt sure, would find a way to blame her, or worse, say she was lying. She wanted to tell his wife, Mrs. Douglas. Surely, she deserved to know what kind of man she was married to. Upon deeper reflection, Sophie surmised that his wife would come to his defense. She had too much invested in her life with him, both emotionally and financially, to rock the boat or face an unpleasant truth.

The Douglases were well thought of in the community. He was a deacon in the church, and Mrs. Douglas organized many of the fundraisers for their local community. Everyone knew Sophie was from the other side of the tracks. It wasn't a secret that her mother was promiscuous. They would assume the apple hadn't fallen far from the tree. She was no stranger to prejudice. It was almost certain she would be judged by her clan and caste, rather than her personal merits. If she told anyone, she alone would bear the shame and defamation of making such an accusation against an "honorable" man. It wasn't like she hadn't seen this kind of thing before. It was a tale as old as time. For the preservation of her own reputation, she decided to tell no one.

A new and deeper level of disappointment crept over her. This latest betrayal was another nail in the coffin of her disillusionment with mankind. It seemed to confirm all her previous conclusions that she couldn't rely on anyone but herself. It almost felt like the whole world was in on a conspiracy that she was not part of—a conspiracy to kill her soul.

She thought of Nana. A flicker of light sprang up inside her chest. She found solace in the thought of her beautiful, weathered face. Yet she wondered why her grandmother hadn't tried harder to intervene on her behalf—

why she hadn't adopted her or taken her away from all this. *If she really cared, why didn't she do something?*

She did not know that Nana had tried to win custody of Sophie. Her dad and grandparents had gone to court, presenting evidence of both child neglect and abuse. They had demonstrated that her living situation was unstable and unsafe. But the courts turned a blind eye to every piece of evidence and testimony. The judge, subject to her own injury and biases, had an agenda of her own, more personal than professional. Rather than protecting the child, her priority proved to be preserving the rights of the biological mother, regardless of her indiscretions.

Sophie could not have known that Nana had tried to win custody, because her grandmother had never told her. Adopting the wisdom of the day, Nana had chosen not to tell Sophie to protect her from complicated, grown-up concerns. However, not knowing had left a void that Sophie filled in with her imagination. Imagining that her dad and grandparents had turned a blind eye, she concluded that she was not worth fighting for.

On occasion, intrusive thoughts of being discarded and insignificant convinced her that she really didn't matter at all. However, all of this was too heavy to ruminate on if she was to keep going. She would not succumb to weakness and victim mentality, as her mother had done. She would prove to herself that she did matter, by being a success. She would find validation in achievements, good grades, and getting that scholarship. There was no time or energy to be wasted on feelings of sadness or loneliness.

Since she was not equipped to process the trauma life had thrown her way, she would continue to cope the best way she knew how. She would store her feelings away, compartmentalize her trauma, find a secret closet in her psyche in which to put it all and firmly lock the door. Nobody would suspect anything. *I'm perfectly fine.*

Sophie doubled her efforts, throwing herself into her ambitions and goals. She got straight A's and was in the running for valedictorian. She spoke with her school counselor and was clear on the specifics of what was required to attain a full ride academic scholarship at her preferred schools. Being a female of ethnic origin was in her favor. She would use it all to her advantage. Being good wasn't good enough; she had to be the best.

As long as she kept a tight rein on her thoughts and focused her attention in very disciplined channels, she was in control. She had little tolerance for trivialities or what she called "fluff." She was a serious person with serious aspirations. She was going somewhere, and if you had nothing of value to offer her, you had best stay out of her way. Her mother was more of a roommate now, her presence an inconvenience that must be tolerated until she could leave this place for a better life. Justine served as a harsh and nauseating reminder of what Sophie was determined never to be.

Sophie had a strong will. She had resolved to take control of her circumstances by being smart and hardworking. She would do whatever it took. She did not understand, however, that her emotional, unconscious mind had a mind of its own. It could not be governed by reason or will. It was governed by emotions, programs, and patterns that were constantly playing out, seeking resolution, and driven to heal childhood wounds.

Meeting Tommy totally blindsided her and threatened to derail everything she had worked so hard to achieve. While Sophie had become a master of managing and suppressing negative emotions, she was not prepared to defend herself—against love.

Chapter 10 -

New Life

Although it felt as if the light had completely gone out of her world, the sun still rose the next day. Madeleine got up as if it were business as usual. What else could she do? She got dressed and reported for duty, putting on a pot of water to start the breakfast routine. For some reason, Hilda's tone was less harsh with her that day, a small mercy.

She went about her morning chores half in, half out of her body. She did not suspect that a new life had begun inside of her.

Madeleine worked harder than she had ever done. She did the most difficult tasks the most difficult way, choosing harsh exposure to the cold without a cloak, washing with scalding hot water until her hands were bright red, scrubbing the floors on her hands and knees with urgent intensity. She attempted to purge the pain inside of her through self-inflicted punishment. But it was never enough.

Small distractions that had once been a reprieve from her monotonous drudgery no longer gave her any pleasure. The joy of going to the market was replaced with dread. She preferred to hide away. *They'll know.*

Days turned into weeks and into months. Her belly was growing, which she found confusing, as she was barely eating. Her monthly bleeding had also mysteriously stopped. No one had ever sat her down to discuss "the birds and the bees." She wanted to ask Hilda about it, but well … you know. Everyone pretended like nothing unusual was afoot so she followed their lead.

She marveled at the strange shape her body was taking on—giant belly with spindly legs. *I look rather like an egg on stilts.* The bigger she got, the less attention she received from the master. It seemed that getting fat was the best thing that had ever happened to her.

The day Madeleine went into labor was a total surprise to the entire household. Apparently, everyone was in denial about her obvious pregnancy. It seemed no one wanted to be the first to mention the elephant in the room, as if hoping it would just magically disappear. Madeleine thought she was dying. Waves of pain unlike anything she had ever experienced wracked her body. She could not have kept quiet even if she tried. This could not be ignored.

"Baby's coming," was all Hilda said.

"Baby?!" Madeleine was stunned. "Oh … baby," she repeated after a long pause, trying to make sense of what was happening. She would have to sort it out later. This was no time for introspection. A baby was coming, and like a runaway train, it could not be stopped.

Hilda assisted her in lying down with her legs up. Hilda was the last person Madeleine wanted to see her like this, much less to be her midwife, but the stabbing pain overrode all sense of modesty or prejudice. She couldn't do this alone, and at least Hilda was here.

Madeleine was in and out of delirium throughout the delivery. So great was her physical pain and so overwhelming her shock in learning what was happening that she dissociated more than usual. She was in and out of consciousness as the birthing process continued all on its own. Somewhere in her dream state, she saw the face of the girl she used to imagine. She looked older now, wiser.

"It's going to be okay," she kept saying. "You're not alone. I'm here to help you."

Several hours of screaming, sweating, and straining later, a baby boy was born. Hilda wrapped him in a towel and laid him on Madeleine's breast. She looked down at him, amazed. She studied his tiny face and fingers. He was perfect.

Looking into her baby boy's soft brown eyes, she whispered, "Hey, you."

It was love at first sight.

Her reverie was interrupted by Hilda asking, "What you going to call him?"

Madeleine thought for a moment. A lineup of the men she had known in her short life scrolled through her mind.

Of course— my dad.

"His name is Steffan," she answered then, connecting once again with the precious thing she held in her arms. "Hello, Steffan. It's nice to meet you!"

The next few days were a whirlwind of learning to breastfeed, holding the baby, changing the baby, rocking the baby, and getting him to sleep. It was under cover of night that Madeleine and Steffan were taken by carriage to a nunnery. Under normal circumstances, the mother would have been forced to give up the infant. However, while the master had little to no compassion for the servant girl, he did possess some sentiment for his own flesh and blood. For the sake of the child, Madeleine would be allowed to keep her baby.

To finally be free of Hilda and her cruel master felt like a miracle. God or the angels must be watching out for her. Madeleine was allowed to spend the first few months of motherhood tending to her baby. Life had become a dream. She did not know to whom she owed her good fortune but she knew it was all happening because of Steffan.

"You're my good luck charm," she told him over and over.

But her staying at the nunnery was a short-term solution. They would not be welcome once the baby was crawling. Madeleine and Steffan would have to leave, but where they would go was uncertain. A single mother had few, if any, options. It didn't matter that she was the victim of sexual abuse, impregnated against her will. To polite society, unwed mothers were considered an affront to morality. Defying all logic, it was as if they were assumed to have conceived on their own, independent of a male counterpart. Women alone bore the blame and the shame.

Madeleine was not completely unaware of her plight. Though ignorant of the ways of the world just a few months before, she was quickly brought up to speed about sex and its consequences. She was faced with many uncertainties. Was she to become a beggar? Would she have to turn to an unsavory profession to avoid starvation for herself and her child? She was certain of one thing: her son was the only reason she had to persevere in her miserable life. *I'll do whatever I have to do to keep him.*

No longer under the servitude of indentureship, she did have some choices, however grim. Her prior situation had all but choked the life out of her. Having Steffan, and tasting even a morsel of freedom, breathed life into her soul. She finally felt like a person.

Time was running out on her stay at the nunnery. They would be thrown out sooner than later. The moment of weakness her former master had felt at the birth of his son had long since passed, his charity and good will expired. Abruptly and without warning, she was led to the door and ushered out, the door locked behind her. Madeleine and her six-month-old were abandoned to the streets.

She wandered to the only place she could think of: the market. She hoped one of the vendors would recognize her and treat her kindly. She found otherwise. Everyone diverted their eyes from her. In such a small village, scandal was impossible to hide, and gossip was their favorite entertainment.

Similar to when her parents had died, everyone was scared to come near her, as if she had the plague. She walked up and down the aisle two or three times before giving up and heading to a different part of town. She found an alley to breastfeed, covering Steffan with her scarf for privacy. The generosity of the nuns had been limited to three rags, which were to serve as diapers and one spare infant gown. She would manage.

As the sun began to set, she noticed men gazing down the alley as if they were looking for something. A man approached her, making direct eye contact.

"How much?" was all he asked.

Madeleine was completely unprepared for his proposition. She quickly calculated the implications, the direness of her situation, and her chances of finding any other means of survival.

"Customary rate," she replied smoothly, although she had no idea what that was.

He motioned for her to follow him. She did so, careful to walk several paces behind him. She followed him into a building and into what she assumed to be his bedroom. Placing Steffan down on the floor wrapped in a blanket, she prayed he would stay quiet.

Throughout the events that followed, she frequently reminded herself that she would do whatever she had to.

Chapter 11

First Love

Sophie was spending more and more time at the library. The chaos at her house was not conducive to studying. The school year was coming to a close, and she only had a handful of exams to get through. The honor of valedictorian had come down to two candidates: Sophie and Seth Peterson. Their scores were within micrometers of each other. A lot was riding on her upcoming exams; her fate hung in the balance. Of the two candidates, she felt strongly that she deserved it more. Seth was admittedly a great student, but he'd had life on easy street compared to her. His parents supported him in every way possible. Sophie had done it all by herself, scratching and clawing for every achievement. Besides, his parents could afford to send him to college. If she was going to get into a top-tier law school, she needed a top-tier scholarship. She needed to win valedictorian and she would do whatever it took.

The library provided an escape from the never-ending stream of drama at home. Justine had deteriorated over the years. Her beauty was waning, and her ability to extort attention from men was becoming more challenging. Her coping mechanisms were wearing thin. Increasingly, she looked to Sophie to fulfill her need for attention and validation.

Sophie didn't have the bandwidth to achieve her personal goals while coping with Justine's demands. As a child, she had longed for her mother's affection. Now the roles were reversed, and she felt herself constantly pulling away, while Justine tried harder to pull her into her orbit. It was suffocating and draining. She knew that if she didn't resist, she would fall into a life as pointless and inane as her mother's. Her stomach churned at the thought.

Her validation did not come from men but from her accomplishments. She sought to be recognized, not for her beauty, but for her brains and diligence. Never did she suspect that, on a deeper level, she sought to satisfy the same need as her mother, to assuage the self-doubt that ever whispered, *I'm not enough.*

Sophie had become a regular fixture at the library, always finding a quiet corner to focus intently on the subject at hand. She came here to study, to work on projects, to fill out applications, and at times, just to reflect. It was her home away from home and felt like her natural habitat.

Tommy worked part-time as a computer tech. He was more handsome than one would imagine a stereotypical library employee to be. He was also friendly and helpful with everyone. Sophie hated to admit it, but she found his boyish good looks difficult to ignore. He possessed an exotic beauty, while simultaneously being extremely inviting and approachable. Frankly, it was distracting, which annoyed her.

Sophie personified the ugly duckling turned into the beautiful swan. In elementary school, she had been awkward, poorly dressed, her hair barely combed, frequently teased by the popular girls. But as time moved on, she had blossomed into a natural beauty. In spite of her striking appearance, on the inside, she still felt like the awkward, unattractive girl she had been before. When she looked in the mirror, she noticed only her flaws, oblivious of her nearly perfect figure. She saw herself as studious, serious, and hard-working, content to dream of love from afar.

Tommy didn't see her that way. He always went out of his way to say hi or ask if she needed anything. It never occurred to her that he was being anything but nice. Sophie frequently stayed until closing.

One evening as they were walking out together, he finally worked up the courage to ask her out on a proper date. "Hey, do you want to go to the movies on Saturday?"

"I should probably study," she replied. "And besides, I'm trying to save up for college."

"My treat, Sophie. I'm asking you on a date," Tommy said, smiling.

Sophie blinked as her mind went on an internal search to interpret what was happening. Tommy, one of the hottest guys on campus, was asking her on a date. Her suspicious, critical inner voice tried to hijack the situation. *He's messing with you. This is a setup.*

After an unusually long pause, she finally managed a reply. "You're asking me on date?"

"Yes. But if you're busy, it's okay."

Tommy Woodbury, the charming, handsome guy who was comfortable talking to anybody and everybody, actually seemed nervous. Sophie felt flustered. She had never been asked on a date before and had no idea how to respond. It wasn't that she didn't want to go—of course, she did. She stood there, staring dumbly, once again reduced to that socially awkward sixth-grader.

"Okay. Yes, I'd like to go on a date with you," she heard herself say. It sounded like someone else was talking in a monotone voice from far away.

"Great! I'll pick you up at six on Saturday." Tommy sounded exuberant as he started skipping away. Realizing he didn't have her information, he yelled after her, "Wait—what's your number?"

"330-867-5309" she yelled back.

Tommy repeated the number back to her to confirm. "Got it! I'll call you tomorrow!"

Sophie walked home in a daze, unsure of what had just happened. *Did Tommy just ask me out on a date? Yes, that just happened.* It was like a land mine had gone off in her brain, opening up a space that just moments before had been neatly filled and perfectly organized with well-thought-out plans for her future. Somewhat disoriented, she felt as confused as she did excited.

Barely responding to her mother's greeting, she walked through the door and went straight to her room, still processing his words and her response. Tucked safely in her cocoon, secure in the privacy of her own thoughts, she finally let herself feel it. *Tommy likes me.*

For the first time that she could remember, a real and genuine feeling of happiness crept into her heart. The words kept going round and round in her head: *He likes me, he likes me..* She drifted off to sleep, a smile on her face.

* * *

The next morning, Sophie woke up feeling as if she had shifted into a parallel reality. Her attention was split, and she was finding it difficult to stay focused on her studies and to-do list. Her almost robotic approach to assignments and responsibilities was compromised. Her heart's emotions were creating an interference pattern with her mind's laser efficiency, slowing her down. What bothered her most was that she couldn't turn it off. She couldn't control these unfamiliar feelings that were invading her consciousness. It was disconcerting.

While she couldn't turn them off, she did manage to rein them in somewhat. It was kind of like placing them in a corral. She placed her thoughts of Tommy off to one side of her mind, up and to the left, like a movie playing in the background, while she continued to do what needed to be done. She got dressed, gathered her books and backpack, grabbed a piece of toast, and headed out the door to school. Today was her political science exam. *You can do this.*

Poli-sci was third period. During her first two classes, she looked at notes for her upcoming exam while the teacher talked. Every now and then, her mind wandered into the corral where she had placed Tommy. Her eyes gazed upwards as she entertained her PG fantasies. *Stop it! Not now.*

She completed the exam feeling more confident than usual. It was more a formality than anything. She had aced all previous tests and knew the material inside and out. Still, she was eager to see how her scores compared to Seth Peterson's. With five exams left to go, she couldn't afford to let her hair down and was determined to put in every minute of study time she could. However, she was faced with a new quandary. She had always gone to the library to get away from distractions, but with the Tommy development, she worried she might be more distracted at the library than anywhere else.

She decided to go the park and study at one of the tables. She could more easily tune out the activity and noise of kids playing than her own thoughts if she were in the same room with Tommy. It was sound logic, in theory. However, Sophie found that Tommy pushed his way into her thoughts no matter where she was or what she was doing. She loved daydreaming about Tommy, but feeling like she wasn't her normal calm and in-control self scared her. She stayed at the park for a couple of hours before throwing in the towel and going home.

As soon as Sophie opened the door, she saw her—face down in a pool of vomit. A combination of panic and rage welled up in her chest. This wasn't the first time her mother had over-dosed.

"No, no, no, no, no, no, NO!" Sophie yelled. Heart racing, she leapt to her mother's side. She turned Justine onto her side, wiping away the throw-up from her mouth and face. She knew to check for a pulse. It was beating. She stared at her chest for signs of breathing. She wasn't dead, thank god. An image of one of her mother's ex-boyfriends doing CPR flashed across her memory.

She grabbed the phone and called 911. In a voice calmer than one would expect from someone reporting a life-threatening incident, she relayed her mother's condition and their address to the dispatch operator. In spite of her deceptively calm demeanor, the image of her mother passed out had caused a full adrenaline dump. As she tried to cover her mother's half-naked body, she noticed her hands were shaking. Everything suddenly seemed far away, like she was at the end of a long hall. A strange buzzing sound filled her ears. She felt dizzy. She heard a voice, but as it was obscured by the buzzing, she couldn't tell where it was coming from.

"Sophie," the voice called. She stood paralyzed, unable to process what was happening. "Sophie, it's going to be okay. You're not alone. I'm here to help you."

The buzzing stopped, her focus returned to normal, her heart rate slowed. She remained standing, staring, not moving. An odd feeling came over her, a sense of knowing something she couldn't possibly know. *Everything's going to be okay.*

In minutes, the ambulance arrived. Sophie gave them a brief history of her mother's medical history and medications. She didn't specifically tell them about her mother's addiction, but it was written everywhere between the lines.

The medics started an IV and gave Justine naloxone, which reversed the effect of the narcotics. She woke up screaming and yelling at them for ruining her high. Sophie watched it all go down, a scene more familiar than she cared to think about. She didn't know if she was more worried about her mother's life, or upset that Justine might threaten her academic future with this latest stunt. Sophie was so tired of the trauma and insanity. She was tired of having to be the strong one, the responsible one, the together one. She was tired, and she was fucking pissed.

Sophie didn't know why she had brought her textbooks to the emergency room, as if she could study here. Her mother's timing was impeccable, creating a crisis to hijack Sophie's attention during final exams. Once again, she would be counted on to pick up the pieces. She wanted to cry from sheer frustration and anger, but the thought of giving in to her own emotions and weakness annoyed her even more.

She sat and waited until the ER doctor came out to explain the plan of care. Protocol dictated determining whether this was a run-of-the-mill overdose or a suicide attempt. They were awaiting a psych evaluation before they could make a decision. It was now after-hours for the psychiatrist, so her mother would be kept overnight at minimum until the eval could be done. Sophie knew the drill.

It was a relief that she wouldn't have to bring her mother home and play nursemaid tonight. These incidents completely stressed her out. It fell on her to make sure her mom didn't do anything stupid or fall back into a drug-induced coma and stop breathing. It was more responsibility than a teenage girl should be saddled with, but when Justine was between boyfriends—which she invariably was when these incidents occurred—there was no one else to care for her.

Sophie now had to deal with the obvious dilemma of what to do with her mother's pills. In the past, she had thrown them out and faced a wrath of fury. It was, of course, the reasonable and responsible thing to do, but the consequences of dealing with her mother's irrational behavior had taught her it wasn't worth it. It wasn't like it would solve anything anyway; Justine would just buy more. So, she gathered them up and put them somewhere her mother wouldn't think to look. She would return them to her once she seemed more stable—stable, of course, being a relative term.

She wondered what would happen to her mother after she left for college, since she had applied out of state. *Maybe I should stay home to take care of her.* She wrestled with a misplaced sense of guilt and felt in a way that her life was not truly her own. The shadow that had been cast over her world since childhood threatened to overtake the promise of a brighter future. *It's not fair!*

At times, she secretly wished her mom would just finish the job. She quickly pushed these guilty thoughts out of sight and out of mind.

As she lay in bed that night, her mind calculating the outcome of every possible scenario, trying desperately to devise a plan that would give her some sense of control, she found a fresh thought gently slipped into the mix. *Tommy.* She had long practiced disallowing feelings of happiness, a subconscious strategy to protect herself from disappointment. But as his face came into her mind's eye, she felt defenseless before the warm feeling that came along with it. It felt too good to push away. She wondered if this was what it felt like to fall in love.

As soon as her alarm went off the next morning, Sophie was up, ready, and out the door, headed to school as usual. She dismissed her concerns about Justine, knowing she was in good hands at the hospital. *Let them take care of her.*

She breezed through her exams. It was as if the answers flew straight from her fingers onto the page. There was really only one thing she was thinking about, and that was Tommy.

When she got to the library, she made sure that he saw her, and that he followed her to her favorite table.

"Where were you yesterday?" he asked.

It flashed across her mind to tell him what had happened to her mother, but she decided that was a little too real. She mitigated her response, saying, "My mom needed me to help her with something."

"How did your exams go today?" Tommy seemed genuinely interested.

"Great!" she replied enthusiastically.

"Beauty and brains," Tommy complimented her. "You're the whole package. We're still going out Saturday, right?"

"But of course." She smiled coyly.

They continued to talk about the weather and grades and high school gossip. Sophie found herself laughing out loud a few times. She genuinely enjoyed his company. He was funny and charming, she had to admit. For once in her life, she decided to just go with it. She feigned trying to study, but succumbed to his teasing and flirting. Anyone who knew her wouldn't have believed she was acting this way. She barely recognized herself. She had never received this kind of attention before. It felt wonderful, exquisite, almost intoxicating. Sophie was under his spell.

* * *

The next few weeks were a whirlwind. She breezed through her finals. Her mother came back home. They had an unspoken agreement to pretend nothing had happened. Sophie still attended her clubs and extracurriculars and worked her part-time jobs—plural—still saving every penny to put towards college. Life was pretty much the same as always—except, of course, for Tommy.

Secretly, Sophie was relieved that her mother was "sick" the day of her graduation, that she would be delivered from the embarrassment of being associated with her. Justine had put on a show of being disappointed, but they both knew she was just hung over. There were no gifts, nor a graduation party. Sophie didn't care. She had given up hoping for her mother's validation long ago.

Tommy was there when she was named valedictorian. He cheered from the audience. He brought her flowers and took her to dinner to celebrate her achievement. Over the next few weeks, they spent as much time as they could together. He introduced her to a slew of new activities. They went for walks and picnics in the park. He took her mini-golfing and she tried indoor ice skating for the first time. He opened doors for her, complimented her taste in clothes, and told her she was beautiful. It was all very romantic.

Tommy was Sophie's first love. Each time he kissed her goodnight, it sent a surge of electricity through her body that left her feeling breathless. This night, they went back to his place. He put a movie on, but they were much more interested in each other. She absolutely adored his kiss. His lips were soft and perfect on hers, his tongue smooth, probing gently. His light touch brought her senses to life. Her body began to respond—her nipples became hard, and she could feel a throbbing in her vagina, driving her to push her pelvis into his. She wanted him.

Sophie had wondered what this moment would be like, if she would know what to do. But as their bodies melded together, nature took over. Tommy had taken his time bringing her to this point. Leaving thought behind, she was taken over by desire. When she took him into herself, it felt satisfying in a way she had never known existed. She took him not only into her body, but into her essence. In the way that only young girls do with their very first, she gave herself to him fully, mind, body, and soul.

For the first time, with the exception of Nana, Sophie felt seen. Tommy was sincerely interested when he inquired about her deepest desires, tender when she shared her greatest fears. When she opened up about her mother, he gently wiped her tears away, kissing her and holding her close. At last, she was not all alone in this world. The comfort of that was beyond words.

Then one day, he didn't call. They had made tentative plans to hang out at his place that evening, but he didn't get in touch with her all day. She tried calling him, but there was no answer. A hollow, empty, scared feeling came over her. It began as a low-level anxiety that built in intensity as the day progressed. *Where is he? Did something happen? Is he okay? Why hasn't he called?*

It felt like her stomach was caving in. An image of herself alone in a forest, lost and cold, flashed across her mind. She was shocked at how fast this awful, sickening feeling had taken her over. Falling in love had been an intense high, but the anguish of being ignored was doubly intense. She had learned to compartmentalize the abandonment and withholding from her parents. She had successfully built a wall around her heart to protect herself from hurt and pain. In a single moment, years of careful construction came crashing down, and her heart was left naked and exposed.

For two excruciating days, Sophie suffered in the hell of not knowing. She envisioned running into his arms and feeling the comfort of his embrace. Oscillating between fear and anger, she concocted imaginary conversations in which he apologized profusely, or she yelled and screamed, demanding an explanation. Fearing the worst, she called the hospital, but no one by his name or any John Doe's had been admitted. She imagined a thousand scenarios and a thousand outcomes. The sick, empty feeling persisted.

Finally, he resurfaced.

"Where have you been?" she demanded.

"I've been busy," was all he offered.

"Busy? Why didn't you answer any of my calls? I was worried sick!" Sophie practically screamed into the phone.

"Calm down," Tommy retorted. "I was helping Max work on his car. It's no big deal. Don't make a federal case out of it."

No more infuriating words had ever been uttered than "calm down." Sophie was livid, but also hurt. She wanted to say, *"I was worried, I missed you, I love you, I need you,"* but she was loath to show that kind of vulnerability when he was acting so nonchalant. Recalling her mother's pathetic displays of weakness, she tried to act indifferent rather than expose her insecurity.

She held the phone for a moment, her mind blank. She literally had no words. Not trusting herself to not say something emotionally charged and needy, she quietly hung up the phone. She had managed to maintain her composure, but inside, it felt like a vice was strangling her heart. A severe and inexplicable pain gripped her. It was a mixture of betrayal, abandonment, and total disregard.

Sophie didn't know what love was supposed to feel like. In songs and in the movies, hundreds of times, she had heard that love hurts. Having had no exposure to healthy relationships, she mistook her feelings of heartache for love. But this wasn't love; it was addiction.

Tommy didn't call her back; he just showed up at her house. She wanted to pretend she wasn't home, but she was too weak to fight the overwhelming yearning to see him. She was in withdrawal, and the only fix to alleviate it was Tommy. He was both the cause and the cure. As soon as he hugged her, her whole body relaxed, and the fight-or-flight response began to subside. Her nervous system went from agony to ecstasy in a matter of seconds. It was reminiscent of the feeling she used to have when her mom would return her attention to Sophie after her most recent breakup. The pain of being ignored followed by the bliss of reconnection was a subconscious program that a part of her had come to enjoy. The warmth of the fire never feels so good as when one comes in from the cold.

Sophie's subconscious pattern of push-me, pull-you, love and rejection was repeating itself. Outside of her awareness, her energy field was broadcasting a unique signature frequency, fraught with insecurity, into the ether. Tommy had tuned into her energy and zeroed in on her signal of vulnerability like a homing beacon. Was Tommy a bad person, or simply acting out the patterns he had witnessed in his own parents' dysfunctional relationship? It didn't matter; the result was the same.

Over the summer, the cycle of hot and cold, on again off again, withdrawal and reunion continued. The rational part of Sophie's mind knew it wasn't right. Tommy oscillated between showering her with attention and affection and cold indifference. He started pointing out flaws in her looks and behaviors, subtle at first, then overtly mean. He made her feel unworthy, reminding her frequently that she was lucky to have him. In constant need of love and validation, she was constantly trying to change herself, to be more and more perfect to secure his approval. He had reduced her to a beggar settling for crumbs. She judged herself for it, but felt helpless to stop it. She felt like she couldn't live without him. It brought her to her knees.

The girl who had carefully cultivated a persona of intelligence and logic had fallen prey to turbulent emotions despite of her best efforts to always remain in control. Under the right circumstances, the wounds of her inner child were activated and hijacked the system. How could someone so smart be so stupid?

Tommy became intoxicated with the power he wielded over her. He had set up the dynamics of their relationship in a way that served him perfectly, with him as king and her as peasant girl. His demands became greater, and she continued to acquiesce, compromising more and more of herself in exchange for a meager allotment of love and affection. Perhaps the only reason he became so controlling was because she let him get away with it. Sophie had not yet learned that we teach people how to treat us.

However, Tommy was a novice. He had yet to perfect his game of narcissistic control and abuse. Fortunately for Sophie, his approach was clumsy and too far-reaching. At first, he tried to get her to give up her dreams of going to university by telling her he loved her and couldn't live without her. When she assured him that their relationship could last through time and distance, he upped the ante with guilt trips, demeaning her and telling her she would never make it.

The summer was not long enough for Sophie to completely lose her sense of self. She had worked very hard to achieve being valedictorian and receiving a full ride scholarship. She not only felt a sense of obligation to herself, but to the faculty and the academic system. Tommy wasn't just asking her to compromise herself, but to betray and let down the people who had invested in her. She felt a strong sense of responsibility and obligation to them. He had gone too far.

In a moment of clarity, a still, small voice inside of her managed to override the noise of her confusion. She heard it loud and clear. *You matter. You have a purpose to fulfill.* It was like a slap across the face. One might have called it divine intervention.

Tommy was used to Sophie being a doormat and did not take it lying down when she decided to stand up for herself. He redoubled his efforts to keep her in her place. Sophie stuck to her guns. She succumbed to neither threats nor pleas, flattery nor insults. It was the most empowering decision she had ever made in her life. She would be going to law school. Nothing would stop her—not her mom, not poverty, not men like Mr. Douglas, not even Tommy. And that was it. She would be leaving in two weeks.

She still felt waves of withdrawal and was tempted to call Tommy a thousand times over the next few days, but she never wavered. She reflected on their tumultuous relationship, the intense infatuation, the heartbreak, and how badly he had treated her. *Such an asshole.* She wracked her brain to find something good that had come of it. She shook her head and laughed. *At least I won't be going to university a virgin.*

Chapter 12

A Friend

Madeleine wandered the streets for a few days, eventually stumbling upon a more agreeable situation. Women like her did not have access to social services. Her condition was viewed as a blight upon society. Charity was favored for widows, not women of ill repute. No one took the time to listen to her story. Nobody cared that she was the victim of injustice. It was easier to simply place her in a class or category without exploring the person behind the label. They saw her as just another unmarried woman with a child, a harlot.

Birds of a feather flock together. While a lot of streetwalkers viewed her as unwelcome competition, others, like herself, still had a sense of civility and saw the benefit of community, however unconventional. Chelsea was a pretty girl with red hair and a sunny disposition. One might expect someone in her situation to be sullen or depressed, but not Chelsea. She had grown up with a father who abused her in every way imaginable. Her mother, a weak and mewling woman, turned a blind eye to his vile and profane behavior. As soon as she had the cognizance and opportunity to run away, she had. Life on the streets was like a vacation compared to what she had endured. Her body was still used by men in some pretty distasteful ways, but at least it was on her terms, more often than not. She was free to agree or disagree most of the time. She was no man's prisoner.

Madeleine and Chelsea hit it off right away. Chelsea showed her the safest alleys, the vendors who were willing to sell to them, and the types of men to avoid. Chelsea was childless and enjoyed the autonomy that came with living and working on the streets. Sophie's situation was different. Having an infant, she needed the protection and safety that shelter provided. Chelsea steered Sophie in the direction of a proper brothel. There were much-needed perks to the situation, although there was definitely some give-and-take.

The primary benefit was a roof and four walls. While humans are highly adaptable and usually find they can do what they have to in order to survive, taking care of an infant came with complications that Chelsea didn't have to contend with. Having somewhere relatively safe to lay Steffan down while Madeleine was working was a tremendous relief and comfort. Naturally, she had to give a percentage of her earnings to the owner of the house, help with cleaning during off hours, and entertain customers she might not agree to work with if given a choice, but it all came, at least, with a small level of safety and protection. She understood Chelsea's choice to be independent, free of bosses or rules, but for Sophie, this was the best choice and she was oddly grateful for her situation.

It didn't take long for Madeleine to find herself in high demand. She was unquestionably prettier than most of the other girls of the house. Her popularity brought in more money for the owner, which gained her certain favors—for example, free babysitting. A less popular girl would be employed to watch Steffan. Everyone at the The Castle, as they called it, loved her baby boy. He connected them to a more normal life. The physical encounters involved in their business weren't exactly of an affectionate or nurturing nature. Having a cute and cuddly baby to hold brought out the mother in all of them. Madeleine had introduced a bright spot into their world, so she was popular, not only with the patrons, but with her housemates as well. In a peculiar way, they were a family. There was certainly more warmth and camaraderie than she had felt in all her years with Hilda and her master.

Steffan grew from baby to toddler to preschooler in the only home he had known. He never lacked for attention, as he was a favorite with everyone from Madam to the girls and even the guests. His presence was most definitely an anomaly, as most children were farmed out to orphanages for a fee, where they were then sold to families or worse—much worse. Keeping Steffan had been a condition of Madeleine's service. Her beauty, her popularity, and the price she fetched—sometimes triple what the other girls brought in—allowed her this preferential treatment. She did not take it for granted. She knew many other women had been forced to give up their babies, a heartbreak she knew she would be unable to bear.

Madeleine and Chelsea continued to hang out a couple of afternoons a week. She was the first and only real friend Madeleine had ever had. She was friendly enough with the girls at The Castle, but she wouldn't truly call them friends. Having seen women come and go, often under duress and involuntarily, they were reluctant to make a serious bond.

Madeleine was on a short leash, her freedoms restricted. In exchange for the safety and security of the brothel, she had to abide by their rules. This meant her visits with Chelsea were monitored and kept short. It was these types of restrictions that motivated Chelsea to risk the streets rather than compromise her autonomy.

On one of their outings, Chelsea told her of some gatherings she had been attending with some women of the village. She invited Madeleine to join her, but didn't offer many details about the gathering itself. When Madeleine pressed her for details, she spoke in vague generalities and alluded to it being of a secretive nature. This sparked Madeleine's curiosity, which, of course, was Chelsea's intention. Madeleine didn't commit, but agreed to consider the offer, if for no other reason than to see why it was so clandestine.

Another reason it piqued her interest was because of Chelsea herself. She had always admired Chelsea's independent nature and her-glass-half full outlook on life. She seemed to have legitimately been born with the happy gene and maintained a can-do attitude no matter what life threw her way. Life had thrown her plenty of adversity, abuse, and trauma that would have broken the spirit of most people. But for Chelsea, it seemed to roll like water off a duck's back. She was injured and hurt by it inside, but she had a resilience and determination that drove her to conquer life rather than be conquered by it.

The fact that Chelsea resonated with these gatherings and vouched for the women who attended them carried a lot of weight in Madeleine's book. While Chelsea was gracious and kind to all, she didn't associate with weak or small-minded people. Madeleine wanted to meet other interesting, self-empowered women who were bold enough to meet in secret. It really meant something to her that Chelsea regarded her well enough to include her. She was intrigued, maybe even inspired, although working out the logistics of time off and childcare would be a challenge. Entrenched in the daily fight for survival, she had little energy or attention left over to spend on loftier goals or ideals. Self-actualization, it seemed, was not easily attainable.

They spent the rest of the afternoon strolling in the park and talking of the sorts of things young girls dreamed of: boys and dresses and far-off places. They swapped stories of good clients and bad clients and outrageous ones.

"I've never seen anything like it, Maddie. There he was, curled up on the floor just begging to be tickled. All he wanted to do was laugh until he came all over himself," Chelsea relayed, laughing hysterically.

Madeleine and Chelsea reveled in the joy of each other's company. An unexplainable synergy made both of them feel happier to be in the other's presence. There was a healing and grounding quality to true friendship. It made life feel safer and friendlier and like it was worth sticking around, despite all the gloomy bits. Madeleine smiled to have such a friend as Chelsea.

Soon enough the afternoon gave way to evening and they had to part ways. Her spirits bolstered, Madeleine gave Chelsea a heartwarming hug.

"You really must come to the gathering," Chelsea implored one last time. "Promise me you'll think about it."

"I promise," Madeleine replied.

And she was gone.

Chapter 13 -

University Life

At university, Sophie found that she was in her element. Serious, academically minded people were the norm rather than the exception. Throwing herself into her studies, she felt more at home than she could ever remember feeling. Here, she was appreciated for her intelligence and hard work rather than treated with disdain for being a brainiac. It was inspiring and frankly a relief to be surrounded by other great minds who shared her interests. She loved being challenged and having intellectual conversations. She had found her tribe.

However, it was definitely more demanding than she had anticipated. High school had been smooth sailing. Back home, she had studied largely because she preferred the company of books to people. Now she studied because she had to. She wasn't the big fish in a small pond anymore. She couldn't put in an average amount of effort and stand head and shoulders above the rest. She had to work for it.

Initially, it was a little disconcerting. It made her question her intelligence of which she had been so confident. Her first B minus on a test threw her into a tailspin. For Sophie, being smart wasn't just a desirable attribute; it was her identity. From birth, life had taken a toll on her security and self-esteem. She had taken solace in excelling in school. Gaining favor and acknowledgement in that arena had earned her a measure of respect and recognition. It was her way of finding her place in the world and feeling good enough. For Sophie, being smart wasn't an option. She had to be smart, so she doubled down and then tripled down.

It began to take a toll. She loved being a part of an elite group of university students and academics, but she was terrified that she didn't quite measure up—terrified that she didn't really belong here. Sophie began to stress-eat.

Food was like a friend that she could count on to be there when she was frustrated or tired or just needed a break from the strain of studying for hours. A few chips here, a little candy there seemed innocuous enough. She was working so hard. Snacks were a much-deserved reprieve. She didn't notice that the pounds were creeping on—that is, she didn't notice until she had trouble zipping her pants one day.

When she looked in the mirror, she barely saw herself at all. She did the basics. Her teeth were brushed. Her hair was combed. Her clothes were clean. She had abandoned makeup a few weeks into the school term. Hyperfocused as she was on her studies, everything else had become extraneous. Unbeknownst to her conscious mind, a subconscious part of her was trying to help her find relief using the only coping strategy it knew: tasty treats.

She hadn't had the time to notice she was starting to fray at the edges. Every day was a battle with homework, papers, and studying for the next exam. It was overwhelming. She had no one to encourage her, no one to coach her or help her put things in perspective. It was her against the world. If she had had a home worth missing, she would have been homesick, but she had nowhere else to go, nowhere else to be. This was it, and she had to succeed.

When she showed up to class looking disheveled and twenty pounds heavier than she had been at the beginning of the semester, Wendy couldn't help but notice. For all of Sophie's efforts to remain invisible, someone finally took the time to stop and see what was happening.

"What the hell happened to you?" Wendy asked, abruptly interrupting Sophie's silence.

Sophie stared blankly, taken aback.

"Are you okay?" Wendy followed up.

"What?" was Sophie's only response.

"You look like you got run over by a bus. Are you okay?" Wendy continued.

"I don't know what you're talking about." Sophie really didn't. No one had ever taken the time to ask her if she was okay before.

"Girl, you need to chill the fuck out. All of this is clearly getting to you. You've gotta take a break. All work and no play makes Jill a dull girl or—in your case, a hot mess," Wendy quipped.

"Yeah, I guess I am pretty stressed out," Sophie admitted, now that she had had a minute to process that Wendy was trying to be friendly.

"A few of us are meeting at the coffee shop across the street after class. You should join us. You need to do something, and I mean anything, besides whatever it is that's got you in this state," Wendy pressed.

"I'm not sure how to take that, but okay," Sophie acquiesced with a smile.

"Great. I'll meet you here after class. And don't flake out. I hate flakes," Wendy added.

Sophie didn't flake out. She waited for Wendy after class, and they walked to the coffee shop on the corner. There she met a group of other wonderful, smart, nerdy colleagues who were all as accomplished and insecure and dedicated and overwhelmed as she was. They welcomed her at once. This eclectic group of individuals were to become both her friends and rivals, cheerleaders and competitors. It was marvelous.

Sophie's stress didn't disappear with her new group of friends, but having people who understood what she was going through helped tremendously. Misery loves company, as they say, and it was comforting to know she wasn't in this alone.

In spite of this, the comfort eating program, once triggered, continued to run on autopilot. As early as the crib, her nervous system had been conditioned, in the absence of nurturing and attention, to accept the bottle as her comfort. With so little happiness to be found in her unfortunate life with Justine, food had continued to be one of the only distractions from loneliness. Wonderful memories of baking with Nana only reinforced her subconscious association between love and food. Eating always made her feel better, but only for a moment. That moment was immediately followed by regret. She was caught in a cycle of a subconscious compulsion to eat to feel better, and a hyper self-consciousness that she was getting fat, which made her feel worse. She would yo-yo back and forth between self-judgment and self-indulgence, feeling more and more confused, worthless, and powerless to change it.

Her ballooning appearance bothered her greatly. Naturally, she didn't want to be unattractive, but even more, she didn't want to be thought of as undisciplined or lacking self-control. The thought of someone looking at her with pity or disdain turned her stomach. She knew that look; she had seen people look at her mother that way. Self-deprecating thoughts of how she looked in her-ill fitting clothes competed with the pressures of assignments and exams. It all made her just want to eat something.

Sophie continued to put in long hours studying. She adapted to the standards and demands of college courses and was once again getting mostly A's with the occasional B. She met with her new study group as often as she could. It was always the highlight of her week. She was beginning to enjoy hanging out with Alex in particular. He was easily the best-looking guy in the group.

"You clearly have a crush on Alex," Wendy taunted one afternoon when no boys were around.

"I do not!" Sophie protested.

Wendy looked at her, eyebrows raised. "Really? Is that so?"

"Well, maybe I do." Sophie laughed. "Is it really that obvious?"

"Only as the nose on your face, darling," Wendy replied wryly.

"Oh my god, that's so embarrassing." Sophie squirmed.

"Not at all. He definitely has a thing for you too," Wendy offered.

"No," Sophie countered. "He would never go for a girl like me. You really think so?" she asked, looking for reassurance.

"I know so. You're not exactly hideous, Sophie," Wendy teased.

Thanks to her brief affair with Tommy, Sophie suspected she might be at least moderately attractive. However, with the extra weight she had put on, she was feeling less than confident. Alex's mere presence made her more self-conscious than ever. She was caught between being magnetically drawn to him and repelled by her fear of rejection.

In a way, being overweight was a way to avoid getting entangled and being hurt again. By convincing herself that she was too fat to put herself out there, she could avoid the risk of heartbreak. However, never putting herself out there ensured she would always be alone. She found herself in a self-created purgatory, motivated both towards and away from food. A cycle of crash diets and bingeing ensued.

Sophie struggled to stay in the safe zone between being pretty and not too pretty. She had learned that being average served to make her more likable to the other girls. Female relationships, she had observed, were a tricky thing. It was a fine line between admiration and jealousy, friendship and competition. A girl might genuinely like her as a person, but add men into the mix, and a strange dynamic emerged. She had noticed a type of catch-22 where women liked having attractive friends because it improved their social status, but if their friend was a supermodel, it made them uneasy. No girl wanted to worry that her boyfriend was secretly fantasizing about her best friend.

Unconsciously, food became a way to keep her in the safe zone of being pretty, but slightly overweight—attractive to men, yet non-threatening to women. Her conscious mind was not privy to this unconscious protective mechanism. All she knew was that she couldn't keep the weight off. The harder she tried, the worse it got, as if the problem kept morphing to outwit her. She beat herself up for not having enough willpower. She did not yet understand that willpower is the weakest part of the mind.

Wendy and Sophie were becoming the best of friends. Beyond being study partners, they were each other's confidantes and partners in crime. They did pretty much everything together. Sophie had never had a true friend since early childhood. It was very grounding. Romantic relationships could be electrifying and intoxicating, but also destabilizing. Friendship was different. It was steady and predictable, like mashed potatoes or toast with jam. Sophie wasn't on the edge of her seat with excitement, but could sink into the couch of comfortableness. It was easy, and it was good.

Sophie didn't yet know it, but Wendy was to become a lifelong friend, one of those rare soul connections that ran through many lifetimes. She could talk to her about anything without feeling judged. She could count on her to be there for her when she felt like crying or raging or eating ice cream. She was there to celebrate her wins and weather her losses. Wendy knew how to just be with her, without having to say anything. She was a gift from the gods.

It wasn't so much what they did together that mattered. It was their spiritual connection that made them so close. Wendy was like an old soul. She neither coddled Sophie when she was tempted to wallow in her victim story, nor judged her for having and expressing a full range of emotions. She provided the perfect balance of empathy and hard-hitting advice, encouraging and challenging her to be her strongest and best self.

As the school year progressed, they saw each other through many of life's ups and downs. Wendy went on a lot of dates with a lot of boys. She was very comfortable with her sexuality and often shared more details than Sophie cared to hear. Sophie was both mesmerized and a little horrified at Wendy's promiscuous affairs. She was free and high-spirited, and something so much more rare: she was happy. Charming and friendly, she could wrap any guy around her little finger. It wasn't that she didn't care about these guys; she just wasn't attached. She didn't need them to validate her in any way. She knew how to make them feel seen and special and wanted without creating any expectations. She seemed to really understand that college was for having fun and exploring her wild side. Sophie envied her ability to squeeze the juice out of life without her own obsessive tendency to constantly second-guess herself. Self-doubt is such a joy-stealer.

Chapter 14

Fools Rush In

Sophie and Alex soon started dating. It wasn't as exciting as Wendy's torrid affairs, but then, Sophie just wasn't wired that way. She was the shy, quiet type, too timid to flirt overtly. Alex played it cool, but Sophie began to notice that when he glanced at her, his eyes lingered a little longer. He leaned in a little closer when discussing an idea. He touched her shoulder gently when getting her attention. He went out of his way to sit next to her, and then he began to arrange private study rendezvous.

Even though she felt self-conscious about her weight, Sophie thoroughly enjoyed the attention. She had been in mild emotional withdrawal ever since she had broken up with Tommy. She often lay in bed at night, fantasizing that he would come to her, blaming himself and begging for another chance. Some disillusioned part of herself still longed to be wrong about him. Her logical mind had been smart enough to walk away from the dysfunction of their relationship, but her heart still wrestled with the fear that she was the failure, that she wasn't enough to make him love her, that it was all her fault.

Alex's attention filled, temporarily at least, the empty space inside of her where self-doubt had been brewing. She felt energized and excited just being around him. He drew her in. The pull of his gravitational field was greater than her ability to resist. When at last they consummated the relationship, she wondered why she had ever resisted. It was like heaven—rich, satisfying, orgasmic heaven.

Giving into desire and togetherness was actually less of a distraction from her studies than the frustration of unfulfilled passion had been. She spent afternoons studying in his dorm room, lying together in his bed and laughing and frolicking like children playing house. Instead of having to find time to be together, they just did everything together all of the time. It felt easy and fun and delicious. It was absolutely wonderful … until it wasn't.

Wendy had issued a few words of warning. It wasn't that she judged Sophie for getting unduly caught up in her situation-ship, but she had definitely noticed cause for concern. Wendy knew who she was and could engage in relationships, connection, and sex without losing herself in the process. She saw Sophie being taken over by Alex like he wanted to swallow her whole.

Wendy saw the red flags, but she was also wise enough to know that unless and until people were ready to hear the truth, it was fool's quest to try to force it upon them. She did feel hurt that Sophie dropped her like a bad habit to spend all her time with Alex, but she was mature enough to know it wasn't personal. Wendy was hurt and disappointed; however, she was a truly rare human being who knew she was responsible for processing her own emotions. She had learned to do this as a child. She grew up with parents who were physically present, but emotionally absent. There were no outbursts, no fighting, no unpleasantries. Everything on the surface was polite and predictable, but a coldness and distance pervaded the air. Wendy was profoundly lonely. Denied comfort and connection, she had found a way to escape into herself.

In the beginning, it happened spontaneously. She would find herself floating above her room, watching what was going on below, as if it were happening to someone else. She didn't know exactly how she did it, but over time, she seemed to be able to will herself to leave her body and travel to other places. On these journeys, she was often surrounded by loving beings that she thought might be angels. She had made the mistake, once, of mentioning this to her mom.

"Those are just imaginary friends," she had been told.

Wendy knew it wasn't her imagination, that it was real, but she was smart enough not to argue the point with her mother. It was her little secret. When out-of-body traveling, she felt a sense of belonging and connection that could only be described as Oneness. It was empowering to realize that she was in control of this aspect of her life. Nobody could add to nor take away from this ethereal experience. She was secure within herself, and she was unshakeable.

After a few attempts to discuss her travels, she had figured out that no one else seemed to have these wonderful experiences. She had access to so much freedom and joy, while her parents were stuck in melancholy and apathy. She felt sorry for them. They were the adults, but she could sense that they were lost and afraid.

Wendy viewed Sophie with that same sense of pity. She knew that Sophie was driven by the same fears and insecurities that controlled the masses. She liked Sophie, and she cared for her, but experience had taught her that she would have to learn some lessons the hard way. She would be there when Sophie was ready. In the meantime, she would continue to live her life to the fullest.

The honeymoon period was great. Alex made Sophie feel accepted and wanted and beautiful. In spite of their limited resources, he found ways to be romantic. They took walks in the park, he read poetry to her in the bathtub, and he took his time in the bedroom. The sex was fantastic. Alex's touch was like rain in the desert. After a lifetime of neglect, physical touch was Sophie's primary love language. Skin-on-skin contact nourished her senses. She couldn't get enough. Great sex and romance blinded Sophie to a host of shortcomings.

It was subtle at first. He made jokes about her flirting with other guys. He made comments about a low-cut top or a skimpy dress. Sophie thought it was kind of cute that he was jealous. It made her feel special, in a way. She didn't pay attention when it started becoming more frequent and less endearing.

Neither Alex nor Sophie had any clue what a healthy relationship was supposed to look like. Her primary reference for love had been the hot-and-cold cycle of attention and withdrawal from her mother. His had been fraught with almost total emotional abandonment. Busy trying to distance themselves from the past, they were disinclined to discuss their childhood trauma. Neither suspected that it had followed them to school.

Chapter 15

Emotional Unintelligence

Alex wasn't able to conceal his deep insecurities or fears for very long. He pretended he was okay and that everything was fine, but when they were alone, he was jealous and angry. If Sophie took issue with any of his bad behavior, he would fabricate an elaborate justification. He assumed that because he was savvy enough to win the argument, it proved he was right. He was articulate, and he was clever, and he bought into his own bullshit.

Sophie was the yin to his yang, the perfect pairing for a trauma bond. Alex wasn't a bad person. He was just an extremely damaged person, and Sophie didn't have the awareness or self-worth to walk away. The subtle red flags started becoming more obvious. Jokes and comments about her interactions and appearance turned into interrogation-style questioning about her whereabouts and the inappropriateness of her attire. To balance the scale of his own insecurity, he tried to make her feel insecure. He could say the most hurtful things.

If Sophie had known what healthy love was, she would have walked away, but her own fear of abandonment prevented her from doing so. His comments struck her to her core. She questioned whether what he said was true. *Am I a slut? Am I a whore?* Alex constantly made her feel unworthy of his love and threatened to withdraw it. They fought, they broke up, and they made up. When he pulled away, she felt a desperate need to win him back, hoping and praying they could return to the way things used to be.

During the breakups, she cried and poured her heart out to Wendy. Wendy listened, patiently at first, pointing out Alex's issues and flaws and frequently reminding Sophie that she deserved better. Sophie would listen and agree and tell Wendy she was right and cry some more.

Then some inane statement would pop out of her mouth. "What if he doesn't take me back?"

Wendy rolled her eyes. It wasn't that she had no compassion for Sophie—she did—but it was hard to watch her be this desperate over an average guy who clearly had issues.

"Why would you want him to take you back? I mean, sure, he's cute, but come on. Stop it, already," Wendy answered, trying to conceal her impatience.

Sophie had become like her mother, ignoring Wendy for weeks at the time when she was entangled with Alex, followed by days of looking to Wendy for comfort and consolation. It was parasitic and gross, but she was too blinded by her own ravaging emotions to recognize it.

Throughout the roller coaster of breakups and make-ups, Sophie managed to keep it together when it came to her classes and studies. From an early age, she had learned to compartmentalize her personal life and hide her emotional turmoil. No one suspected a thing. She showed up to class, was pleasant and responsible, and by all appearances had her act together. For Sophie, studying was her one foolproof distraction. Rather than escaping from her responsibilities, she escaped into them.

Alex kept their troubles away from the attention of others too. He was just as motivated as she was to keep up the facade that all was well in paradise. The only person who knew any different was Wendy. They looked like the picture-perfect couple, always seen smiling and laughing, showing off their blissful romance, the envy of all. They were a striking couple and attracted attention everywhere they went. Alex loved the social status of having a hot, charming girlfriend, but Sophie always paid the price for being friendly and beautiful. While a part of his ego thrived on the attention he got by proxy of having such an attractive girlfriend, another part of his psyche got triggered every time another guy so much as looked at her. If she spoke to any member of the opposite sex for any reason in any context, there would be hell to pay.

Alex had been betrayed by his primary caregiver. His mother often sent him to his room for hours or even days, withholding all human contact. The terror of being alone was visceral and had settled into every fiber of his nervous system. The slightest offense, real or imagined, could trigger a full-blown fight-or-flight response. It wasn't that he didn't trust Sophie specifically, but she was the person he had given access to his heart, which gave her the power to hurt him. She became the surrogate villain in his story of betrayal and injustice.

With the same intensity with which he verbally attacked her and pushed her away, he would cling to her and beg her to stay. Sophie couldn't bear to leave him when he needed her so badly. His desperation made her feel significant. If he couldn't live without her, then it proved to her that she really mattered. She needed to be needed as badly as he needed her.

Alex inflicted pain on Sophie to mitigate his own. He knew her insecurities and targeted them with lethal precision. While she was stunningly beautiful, he knew she wasn't happy with the weight she had put on. His comments struck Sophie to her core. She couldn't stand what she saw in the mirror. She looked at her belly and thighs and found them repulsive. *Why would Alex want you? You're fat and disgusting.*

Sophie secretly began to purge. She had heard of other girls doing it and hadn't understood it at the time. But now it seemed like the perfect solution. She could eat whatever she wanted, then simply rid her body of the consequences. It was the perfect solution in other ways too: it served to purge her self-loathing and to punish herself for not being perfect. She knew it was dysfunctional, but she justified it as a life hack or a shortcut, a simple way to solve a difficult problem. This became another secret she kept hidden away. She began to develop a relationship with this part of her life and enjoyed it almost as much as eating. She looked forward to the feeling of ridding herself of what she could neither give up nor bear. After each occurrence, she felt cleansed and purified.

Even Wendy didn't notice what was going on. She had distanced herself emotionally when Sophie began to get entangled with Alex. She still made time for her and listened and counseled her, but she had taken a step back as far as her own emotional investment went. It was a few months before she even realized that Sophie had lost weight. *She's lost quite a bit of weight, actually.*

Wendy complimented her on how good she looked. Sophie shrugged it off, feeling conflicted about her methods and reticent to acknowledge Wendy's observation. She had lost the weight, but it didn't make her feel any better about herself. She was deathly afraid someone would figure out what was going on. It was embarrassing to be seen as fat, but it was equally distressing for anyone to notice she was getting thin. She would rather be invisible.

When Wendy finally figured out that Sophie was losing more weight than could readily be explained by diet and exercise, she started investigating. Wendy was one of those rare people who could pull off asking the hard questions without making you feel defensive. She personified love and non-judgment. Her energy of unconditional acceptance superseded any fear of criticism. It wasn't Wendy's questions that made Sophie feel vulnerable, but her compassion that was her undoing. She could feel her empathy and genuine care. It was hard to take.

Sophie held back her tears, knowing that if she let down her guard, even to Wendy, her whole house of cards would come crashing down. She wasn't ready to ask herself the kinds of questions Wendy was asking. She wasn't ready to look at herself and see what was really going on. She preferred to keep pretending that everything was okay, that she and Alex were happy and that she was just too busy to eat.

"Don't make me take you to the doctor before you disappear altogether," Wendy said with a laugh. They both knew she wasn't joking.

Alex's emotional abuse didn't miss a beat when Sophie began to lose weight. Her improved figure and sexy physique drove him mad with jealousy. She was constantly forced to apologize for things she hadn't done. Nothing she could say or do was enough to appease the green-eyed monster.

He knew her dark secret, and he knew the exquisite pain it caused her. His cruelty matured in its sophistication. He shifted his focus from targeting her body image to shaming her very personhood. He reminded her daily that her bulimia was vile and disgusting. He made her feel ashamed and bad about herself on a fundamental level.

Sophie just wished things could go back to the way they were when they first met. *We were so happy.* She held onto the honeymoon of the past and a fantasy of the future while enduring the pain of the present.

"You should never date a guy's potential, Sophie," Wendy told her. "Just because he could be a great guy doesn't mean he's ever going to be."

"I know, I know," Sophie weakly agreed.

Wendy knew that Sophie would leave when she had suffered enough, but Sophie's capacity for suffering seemed to know no bounds. She remained in the hell she had chosen for an exorbitant amount of time. She was nothing if not resilient.

It didn't seem that Sophie had the sense or the courage to end the madness. Her higher self had watched it go on for far too long. An exit strategy would have to be orchestrated on her behalf. She was soon to learn that the best gifts often come in the worst way.

Sophie walked in on them in his apartment. Her afternoon classes had been canceled due a power outage in the building. By some small mercy, she didn't catch them in the proverbial act. She was spared seeing the burning image that couldn't be unseen. When Sophie opened the door, Alex and the other girl were sitting on the couch, engaged in intimate conversation.

The girl looked nervous and guilty as she introduced herself. Alex's expression was a mixture of anger at being caught and triumph in exacting revenge for her imagined transgressions. He offered a flimsy explanation that they were studying and had come back to his place to fix something to eat. But there was no evidence of food or its preparation.

Sophie was stunned. In all of the scenarios she had played out in her mind of where her life with Alex would wind up or how their story would end, this was in none of them.

The full scope of the insanity of their so-called relationship was illuminated like a bright, flashing neon sign. All of the denial and coping mechanisms she had employed to pretend to herself that Alex was her knight in shining armor dissolved in that single moment of perfect clarity. There was no ground beneath her, no sky above her, no walls around her. She felt herself in a great void of nothingness, alone but proud.

She processed every detail of the last many months in an instant. She knew instinctively that there was only one thing to do. She gathered her things, placed them in a trash bag, and walked right back out the door. Anything that needed to be said had already been said a thousand times over without ever once being heard. There were no words left. He was not worth the breath it would take to utter them.

Chapter 16

Moving On

Sophie did not look back. She had stood in the middle of the hurricane that was Alex, the world spinning around her, for two years. She had wasted her college years, socially at least. Graduating with honors, she received offers from several of the most prestigious law firms in the country. In that sense, her university career was a huge success, but she had missed out on the fun and adventure of college life. She regretted what she had allowed to be taken from her, but she couldn't have done anything differently. Alex had been a painful but necessary part of her journey.

Sophie put her big girl pants on and kept moving forward. She had many interviews and received many offers. In a way, it was more like she was interviewing them. As top of her class, she was the most desirable candidate—on paper, anyway—and they all seemed eager to roll out the red carpet.

She was in for a bit of a surprise to find that the good old boys culture was still alive and well. Naively, she had assumed that she would be judged on the basis of her merits alone. She was not prepared to be discriminated against, secretly and silently, for being a woman. She would certainly be given a job by someone, somewhere, but it might not be the one she wanted, and it might not be for the reasons she had hoped. Some viewed her as their way to meet the minority quota. Others saw her as a way to improve their image in the community. Few, if any, saw her as lawyer first and woman second.

One thing was certain: she was not seen as an equal. She was treated differently. She was not part of the club. It seemed that, because they had written the book on sexual harassment, it somehow made them exempt from its implications. She maintained her composure and acted as if she didn't even notice the subtle sexist remarks. She pretended to laugh when they implied there were dubious reasons for her graduating top of her class.

"I bet you were on top," one guffawed.

Inside, Sophie rolled her eyes, but outwardly, not even a hint of displeasure flickered across her face. *Does this pig really think I went to college and got a degree as some form of elaborate sexual role-play? I'm not here to be your sex kitten, asshole.* It was infuriating.

"Good one," she said, playing along.

She had worked too hard and come too far to be thin-skinned or let a few unpalatable remarks be her demise. She would suck it up and let it roll off her back. To be honest, compared with the abuse and injustice she had suffered at Alex's hands, this mild form of mistreatment wasn't that big of a deal. Sure, it wasn't right and it wasn't fair, but she had learned long ago that life wasn't fair. She was a realist and knew that in order to extract what you wanted from the system, you had to deal with circumstances as they were, not as you wished them to be.

That said, she wasn't going to jump at the first offer she received. She knew her value, even if they didn't, and she wasn't prepared to sell herself short. She interviewed with several high-ranking firms and was pleasantly surprised to consult with another female attorney. Brigette was professional and pleasant and seemed eager to have her join their team. Sophie was thrilled to have found a female mentor and colleague.

Over the next day or two, as she weighed her options, she knew how lucky she was to have these kinds of choices. As hard as she had worked, she still felt some unworthiness tugging at her. She felt like an imposter. *What if they find out I'm just some poor girl with an alcoholic mother, pretending to be an upper-crust attorney?*

Part of her wanted to choose the top firm to prove to everyone that she was good enough, but another part of her felt intimidated to try to live up to those expectations. The added bane of chauvinistic men constantly trying to hold her in a position of inferiority felt intolerable. It was a tough decision. She called the only person she could trust for impartial advice: her Nana.

Daisy was still living in the same little house where Sophie had visited her for two weeks each summer growing up. Sophie had tried to keep in touch whenever she had the time, however, the demands of school and the drain of her relationship with Alex meant her biweekly phone calls had dropped to a couple of times a year. Daisy never complained or tried to make Sophie feel guilty, which was always the main thrust of her conversations with her mother. She genuinely dreaded talking to Justine, who mostly talked about her problems or her latest dating fiasco.

"Why don't you ever come see me? Don't you love your mother anymore?" she would inevitably say, resorting to familiar guilt tactics and ploys for attention.

"You know I'm busy, Mom," Sophie would find herself defending, still under the psychological spell of her mother's manipulation.

It was too much. Her mother would never be able to comprehend the effort and discipline it took to accomplish anything, much less becoming a lawyer and studying for the bar. The only reason Sophie called at all was to avoid a bigger guilt trip if she put it off too long.

By contrast, talking to her Nana was always a breath of fresh air, and she always hung up wondering why she didn't call her more often. As soon as she picked up the phone, it was like she had just spoken to her the day before. Their connection was timeless and effortless. She spent a few moments catching up on what had been going on with the dog and the cat and what vegetables she had planted in her garden this year. Her voice felt like soothing rain drumming a windowpane while cuddled up on a cozy afternoon. As she talked, Sophie pictured her smiling face and her warm yellow kitchen. She could almost smell her famous chocolate chip cookies. Even the sound of Nana's voice felt like home.

Daisy could sense that Sophie had something on her mind.

"What's going on, Princess?" She had always used this term of endearment, ever since Sophie used to play dress-up. It made Sophie smile to remember her castle tent and tiara.

"Oh, Nana," Sophie sighed. "I need your advice."

Sophie proceeded to tell her far more than she had planned on divulging. Daisy provided a safe space for her to finally let her guard down and talk about the pain and betrayal she had experienced with Alex. She felt tears welling up, something she normally hated, but she could finally allow the full depth of her feelings to come up and out while on the phone with her Nana. She had been too embarrassed to tell Wendy about how bad it had gotten towards the end. Feeling the love on the other end of the line, she broke down and sobbed. She had been so strong, but it had been so hard, and she was exhausted. Daisy sat quietly, holding space for her to let it all out. Eventually, the sobs slowed, then stopped.

Sophie laughed from the relief she felt and jokingly said, "Well, that was unexpected. What is it about you, Nana, that always makes me cry?" She paused, then added, "I love you."

"I love you too, Buttercup." Buttercup was another favorite nickname of hers. Since her grandmother was named after a flower, Sophie had wanted to be a flower child too.

Sophie felt a huge weight lifted after getting so much repressed emotion off her chest. She took a deep breath and explained the ins, the outs, and the what-have-you's of the decision she faced. The list of pros and cons had spun round and round in her head like a merry-go round, but she never got any closer to reaching a conclusion.

Daisy understood the limits of the logical mind and invited her to consider looking at it from a different perspective. She guided Sophie to close her eyes and picture, one at a time, being in each office building, sitting at her desk, interacting with her colleagues and taking clients. While picturing herself there, Daisy instructed her to scan her body and tune in to how she felt. Did she feel light? Did she feel heavy? Did she feel happy or oppressed?

Sophie humored her Nana and played along. She was surprised to notice that the feeling was palpably different in each scenario. She was even more surprised to find that the feeling was significantly better and more positive when she pictured herself working at the top firm with predominantly male partners. She hadn't expected that and was caught a little off guard. *That can't be right. It's just a silly exercise.*

In any case, taking a few minutes to get out of her head and into her heart was grounding, like she was tuning into the truth of who she was for the first time in a very long time. Her Nana always had this effect on her. She felt a profound sense of peace. She took a deep breath and let it out with a sigh.

"Thank you, Nana."

"My pleasure, Princess."

They talked a while longer and finished their conversation. Right before they hung up, Daisy added, "Don't be a stranger."

Sophie sat, feeling oddly happy and connected to life. Her grandmother had forged a tiny opening in her wall of self-protection. She felt her presence long after she hung up the phone. She had missed her more than she realized. It was a lovely reminder that there was some softness, some goodness in this world of hard edges and forcefulness. As she drifted off to sleep that night, she floated in an ocean of love, its warm water gently lapping, caressing, holding her. It was lovely.

* * *

When she awoke the next morning, the wonder of her conversation and connection had faded. The clarity she had felt with such surety was once again clouded with analytical questions and self-doubt. As much as she loved and trusted her Nana's heart and intentions, she convinced herself that what she had felt the night before was just a bit of silliness. Tuning into your body and feelings was a quaint and naive approach to solving problems, certainly not logical in any way.

She discounted her own experience and deferred to her intellect, as she was accustomed to doing. She was familiar with relying on logic and reason. She was comfortable with this way of doing things, and to be fair, it had served her many times in the past. But there are times when we don't know what we don't know, and this was one of those times.

Chapter 17

The Professional

Seeking the reassurance of the familiar, Sophie got back in her head and deferred to her checklist of pros and cons. While control is an illusion, the perception of control can be extremely seductive. The subconscious and emotionally driven reason Sophie decided to go with the firm where she had been interviewed by the female partner was because she didn't quite believe she was good enough or could meet expectations at the top firm. She convinced herself, however, that it was for noble reasons, namely that she couldn't support a company who treated women as second-class citizens, and that she couldn't, with a clear conscience, represent them. This conclusion served her sense of moral superiority quite well. The ego is a sneaky little devil.

She made her decision, and she tactfully and professionally explained her choice to her peers, being careful to feign concern rather than disdain for the shortcomings of the establishment she had rejected. Having mastered doublespeak and innuendo, she was able to wordsmith and deliver a proper and civil critique while making sure her point was not missed. She was a lawyer, after all.

Sophie didn't take any time off before she started to work. She was welcomed on board with a great deal of enthusiasm and accolades. Her résumé spoke for itself. She was qualified and talented, so they wasted no time assigning her first case. It was a simple assignment—or so they led her to believe. On paper, it looked straightforward, but Brigette knew something Sophie couldn't have. It wasn't the case that was complicated; it was the personalities involved that could and would make it convoluted and complex. She had worked with these clients before, and she knew how impossible they were. She smirked, almost imperceptibly, when she handed the file to Sophie. It was a little initiation they liked to call "trial by fire."

Sophie was eager to get started and prove herself capable. It was a small case, but she threw herself into it with commitment and pride. But it didn't take long for her to discover the unsavory nature of her clients. They constantly changed what they wanted and were never satisfied. They seemed to have no respect or regard for her expertise, but rather ordered her about like she was their hired help. She couldn't get through to them that their demands would be seen as unreasonable by any judge. To acquiesce to their demands was to embarrass herself in the court-room, something she couldn't afford to do. It was a no-win situation, and she needed a win.

She could not believe it was all starting out this way. And rather than give her support or guidance, Brigette only laughed at her frustration.

"Welcome to the jungle," she sneered. Sophie could see the gleeful mischief in her eyes, noting that Brigette made sure to confront her in front of the whole team. "So, how's the Dawson case coming along?"

"Oh, it's coming," was all Sophie would reply.

These little zingers were all the confirmation she needed to know that this was a setup. She had been wrong about Brigette. She wasn't a female ally in a male-dominated world. She had been used to sway Sophie to choose their firm above the others. She was good at what she did and had successfully lured her in, but she was not her friend. Unfortunately, like too many women, Brigette saw her as her competition, a threat rather than a confidante.

Sophie's heart sank at her realization that she had made the wrong choice. Working here was going to be an uphill battle. Her success would be undermined in subtle and covert ways, her competence brought into question in secret meetings behind closed doors, all handled with the same civilized and masterful wordsmithing that she herself often wielded.

It wasn't that Sophie wasn't up for the challenge. She knew how to work hard and overcome adversity. Her whole life had prepared her for this. She would do whatever it took, and she would be a success. It was just going to be more exhausting and less enjoyable than she had hoped. The payoff for getting through school and becoming a lawyer seemed more bitter than sweet. The carrot of true fulfillment still dangled just out of reach.

Since high school, teachers, counselors, and peers had assured her that good grades, a college degree, and high-status job would bring the happiness she had been seeking. She had achieved the trappings of success, a high salary and status, yet it had turned out to be a hollow victory. If she had had the time to ask herself if she was happy, the answer would have been an unsettling no. Sophie acquiesced to being a cog in the wheel of society, albeit a very well-educated, well-paid cog.She had written off the pursuit of happiness as the stuff of fairy tales, the American dream sold to motivate people to achieve more. Sipping brandy at the local pub with a group of yuppies, she sounded off on the futility of striving for happiness.

"Really, Carter, I mean, what would happen to society if everyone was innately happy and satisfied with the way things are? No one would ever do anything, ever. Society, as we know it, would simply fall apart. Don't you think so, Roland?"

"I wouldn't dream of arguing with you, Counselor," Roland jested.

"Besides, no one's happy. Do you know anyone who's really and truly happy? It's all a scam," Sophie continued. She knew this was a lie; Nana and Wendy were legitimately happy human beings. *They don't count. They were born with the happy gene.*

"Well, I, for one, am supremely happy to be sitting here having drinks with the esteemed Sophie Davenport, legal eagle extraordinaire," Roland pivoted.

"I suppose that would make most men happy, you lucky dog," Sophie flirted, letting the topic go.

Sophie's life was mostly consumed with work and clients and cases and settlements and court and winning as often as possible. It was a lot, and it left little time for a personal life. Dating was nearly impossible. Finding a man of her caliber felt like mission impossible. She made her checklist of desirable qualities. Years later, she would realize this list was rather superficial, but at least she had a list, something she had never even contemplated when she had stumbled into her previous relationships.

She met Robert at a networking mixer for entrepreneurs and young professionals. He was charming and handsome, professional, and well thought of in the community. Indeed, he seemed to check all the boxes.

Robert felt no need to observe social taboos. Confident and self-assured, he flirted with Sophie shamelessly, making no apology for his not-so-subtle advances.

It had been over a year since Sophie had felt herself respond to a man this way. At work, she maintained a calm, cool demeanor, politely brushing off any attempts at chumminess or personal conversation. She prioritized gaining the respect of her associates and wanted it to be clear that she was there to work. Mixing business with pleasure not only made things messy, it was sure to diminish her reputation. The patriarchy always made sure that women took the fall. She would not make that mistake.

Robert, however, was fair game. He was clean-cut and professional, and best of all, he was not a lawyer. After so many months of keeping her guard up at all times in every situation, she felt the little girl in her peeking out from behind the curtain. It felt so good to get in touch with her feminine side. She found herself flirting back, shyly at first, but soon she came out of her shell.

He made her feel pretty and attractive and sexy all at once. In his presence, she lit up like a Christmas tree, all smiles and laughter. She let him touch her hand, wishing he would grab her and kiss her. The way he made her feel had an intensity that was all too familiar, and she had missed it. She had repressed her sexuality and emotions for a full year, carefully maintaining her persona as intellectual, logical, and disinterested. As if a switch had flipped in her brain, she wanted to feel good, whatever the cost—and she wanted to feel good now.

Sophie went home with Robert that night. It felt good to indulge in consensual sex without guilt or hang-ups. That was something she had learned from Wendy—to be free and comfortable with her own body and her own appetites. It was as liberating as it was delicious. *I'm back, baby.*

For a brief period, Sophie surrendered to a torrid affair with Robert without any attachment. His lighthearted and easy manner felt refreshingly honest and natural. She had never been around a man who didn't have an agenda of some kind. She was welcome to sleep over or leave. There was no pressure, no expectations. They ate and watched TV and laughed in bed.

"I don't believe I've ever laughed in bed before," Sophie commented.

"Well, that's a damn shame," Robert responded. "You do like laughing, right?" he said, pretending to be serious.

"Hate it," she professed, and he proceeded to tickle her.

Life with Robert was comfortable and simple, like coming home. Without even trying to, he was teaching her neurology what calm and happiness felt like. His energy was unwinding some of the twisted patterns in her mind and releasing some of the dark energies in her aura. He was the first man she had ever met who seemed to know who he was. He had nothing to prove, no need for power struggles, domination, or mind games. Robert was an anomaly—a miracle, really.

Their affair ended almost as quickly as it had started. He was being transferred out of state with his company. They both intuitively knew that trying to navigate the complications of a long-distance relationship would only tarnish the beauty of what they had shared. Some of life's gifts were best left unspoiled, to be held in one's heart as a perfect memory.

In a sense, Sophie lost Robert when he drove away, but she would never lose the impact he had made on her life. Breathing life back into her bleak and empty world, he had shown her that pure joy and love were possible. Robert had been one of life's little surprises. Even the ache he left in his absence served as a sweet reminder that he had been there. She had no regrets.

Recharged in mind, body, and soul, she threw herself back into her work with renewed vigor. Her productivity skyrocketed. Everyone at work noticed that she was more confident, self-assured and efficient—especially Brigette. The whole office staff was warming up to Sophie. Brigette's put-down tactics weren't working anymore, and no one laughed at the jokes she made at Sophie's expense. *My, how the tables have turned.*

When Sophie had a few minutes of downtime or was waiting for a client, she would find herself staring out the window, reminiscing about Robert. A smile would come to her face. Just knowing he was out there made the world seem like a better place. Her mind wandered to the other good souls she knew who made the world a better placed. *Wendy!*

She hadn't spoken to Wendy since the Alex fiasco. Sophie rolled her eyes and shook her head. *I can't believe I wasted so much time with him.* She had known at the time that Alex had placed a wedge of sorts between Wendy and herself ,but she trusted Wendy to let bygones be bygones. If there was one person who would appreciate her affair with Robert, it was Wendy. Feeling nervous, she gave her a call.

Wendy was genuinely happy to hear from Sophie. She was working with high-end real estate clients. She lived in California. The weather was wonderful. As expected, it sounded like she was on top of the world, and everything was going her way. They spent nearly two hours on the phone, catching up on everything from cases to co-workers to dating and anything else they could think of. When Sophie told Wendy about Robert, she heartily congratulated her.

"That is fabulous! Good for you. Sex is very life-affirming," Wendy said emphatically.

Sophie had never heard it put into words before, but she had to agree. "Yes. Yes, it is," she responded. She had known she could count on Wendy to appreciate the beauty and significance of her experience without diminishing it or judging it.

"You should come visit," Wendy invited.

"'Oh my god, that sounds so amazing!" Sophie replied with a sigh. "Man, I wish I could…" she trailed off. She could really use a getaway, but she was still low man on the totem pole at the firm, and it would be nearly impossible to negotiate a vacation.

Wendy knew what was going on in Sophie's mind without her verbalizing it. "Anyway, it's an open invitation. Come whenever you like, or whenever you can," she added.

They finally managed to pull themselves away from the phone after chatting like school girls. Sophie was so glad she had mustered up the courage to reach out. It felt like old times, before Alex, and before life had become so serious. It felt good to have an authentic female friend that was on her side. Most of all, it felt good to be in touch with that part of herself again.

Chapter 18

The Gathering

Madeleine could not stop thinking about the gatherings Chelsea had told her about. *I wonder what they do and why it's such a secret.* Her curiosity was definitely getting the best of her. Life kept her busy and preoccupied most of the time, but the thought of it was always there, off to the side, like a mosquito that didn't land but wouldn't go away. When she lay down at night, it came to the surface of her mind with vivid images of these women having parties and laughing and dancing gaily. Oddly, she felt left out.

She met with Chelsea once every fortnight near the town square. Her curiosity would not be satisfied until she saw her next. She made a mental list of questions to ask her. Her life, thus far, had held very little wonder. Practically nothing out of the ordinary ever occurred, certainly nothing with the promise of surprise and fascination. It awoke a feeling in her that she barely recognized—a feeling of expectation. She couldn't wait to see Chelsea again.

When Thursday came, she was antsy and impatient. She got up early and finished all of her house duties in record time. She got herself and Steffan dressed and was sitting on the bed, anxiously waiting for the minutes to tick away. Steffan played with a couple of toys on the floor. He was almost old enough to play outside by himself, but Madeleine wasn't comfortable with the thought of him being unattended. She had little trust in humans. As a child, she had suffered at the hands of ruthless adults. It was not uncommon for children to be snatched up off the streets, used for child labor or traded into indentured servitude She was intimately acquainted with that horror. She kept Steffan close, preferring he stay inside, within earshot.

Madeleine had gotten him ready far too early, and now they were all dressed up with nowhere to go. She sat, tapping her foot. Steffan was getting bored. She rearranged the knickknacks on his dresser, brushed her hair again, fidgeted with her clothes, and tried on several bracelets. When she couldn't take the anticipation another minute, she grabbed Steffan by the hand and left the building.

"You're leaving early, ain't ya?" one of the girls, who liked to consider herself enforcer of the house rules, questioned.

"Well, I've done all my chores. What's it to ya?" Madeleine replied.

She was early, but it was definitely better to walk around the town or market than to sit anxiously waiting. At any rate, it would give her a chance to show off Steffan. He was very polite and social, always a crowd pleaser. They visited a few shops and vendors, wandered the market, and stopped to buy him a piece of rock candy.

Chelsea always managed to add a splash of color to her attire, which made her stand out in the crowd. Spotting her from all the way across the square, Madeleine waved enthusiastically the moment she saw her. They greeted each other with a hug, and as always, began talking excitedly, often talking over each other.

"So, what is this gathering all about? You must tell me. I've been going mad with curiosity!" Madeleine blurted out loud, unable to stand it a minute longer.

"It's kind of hard to explain," Chelsea replied vaguely.

"Don't be so mysterious. Tell me," Madeleine demanded.

"I'm not trying to be annoying, really," Chelsea replied. "It truly is difficult to explain. It's like trying to describe what a gooseberry tastes like to someone who has never had one. It just tastes like a gooseberry. What I can tell you is that we practice different forms of what one might call divination. We are seekers, searching for guidance from the metaphysical realm."

Madeleine realized that Chelsea was right: she did not understand what she was talking about. She didn't have a reference for the terms *divination* or *metaphysical*. She couldn't comprehend what Chelsea was saying mentally, but intuitively she knew that this was something important. She felt a stirring inside of her like an enlivening of her soul, the call of destiny.

"We meet on the full moon in the grove of trees by the river," Chelsea said. "Make sure you come alone," she insisted.

Madeleine could hear the serious tone in her voice. She felt a chill run up her spine when she considered the consequences of being found out by pious and judgmental religious leaders.

The full moon was less than a week away. Madeleine would have to call in a favor from one of the girls at the brothel to watch Steffan while she slipped out. It seemed juvenile that a working woman should have to sneak out of her own abode, but the madam of the house had strict rules, and there were serious penalties for not abiding by them. It was definitely risky. But a handful of the prostitutes had created an alliance. They covered for one another and could be counted on to keep their mouths shut in this type of situation. These women formed a sisterhood of sorts. They weren't the kind of friends you could trust with your deepest, darkest secrets, but Madeleine could rely on them because they, in turn, relied on her. If they betrayed her, it would be their own undoing.

She arranged to leave about an hour after nightfall. One of her friends distracted the madam while another flirted with the security guard. Madeleine slipped down a dark alley and headed out of town. She knew the area well, so she had no difficulty making her way, even in the dark, to the location Chelsea had described. The trees were thick, so she didn't see their lanterns until she was almost right upon them. As she stepped into the cleared area, Chelsea walked towards her and greeted her with a kiss on the cheek.

"This is Madeleine," she announced.

"Welcome Madeleine," they all chimed in together.

There was a fire in the middle of the clearing. The main speaker stood in front of the other women, who formed a semicircle. She wore a hooded cape, and the firelight on her face gave her the glow of a mystic. She recited some prayers and incantations, which sounded very foreign to Madeleine. The mood was reverent. The women seemed to have a great deal of respect and admiration for her. She held a glass ball in her hands. As she spoke, the wind began to move in the trees as if responding to her words. Madeleine could feel something in the air—an energy she didn't recognize. She felt a shiver go up her spine and goosebumps break out across her arms.

Without warning, the priestess's eyes rolled back in her head, and her body began to shake. All were silent. Then she began to speak, but her voice sounded completely different. Madeleine would later learn that she was channeling.

"You are the bringers of the light. You are a blessing to all men. You are surrounded by many guides and you have been watched over since the day you were born. Your guides are here to assist you in your mission to anchor divine love and light onto the Earth plane. Remember who you are."

The wind blew through the trees once more. The priestess, as Madeleine thought of her, once again shuddered, and her eyes returned to normal. When she spoke again, it was in her own voice. She looked slightly dazed and drained from the experience. Several women rushed to her side to offer her support and a cup of wine. She sat, motioning for the others to join her.

The evening continued with a history lesson on the teachers who had gone before, their connection to the earth, their relationship with spirit, and how they had been persecuted by many groups and leaders throughout many time periods. They carried sacred knowledge to benefit all people, but they were seen as a threat to those who preferred to enslave humanity rather than free it.

The women broke into small groups to practice bone-casting and tarot readings, with those who had been attending longer teaching the newer members. There was so much to learn, and it was all so fascinating. Madeleine heard them talk of mediums and table-tipping and scrying.

Before she knew it, it was time to go. The women put out the fire and carefully hid any evidence of them having ever been there. They were given a reminder to use discretion in keeping their gathering a secret and to vet any potential new attendees with vigor. With that, the gathering was over.

The evening had been a whirlwind of new information and new experiences. Madeleine left feeling inspired, like she was connected to something bigger than herself, like she was a chosen one whose life had a purpose beyond her mundane existence. She hadn't known it, but this was what she had been searching for her whole life. As she lay down on her bed, her hands on her heart, she gave silent thanks to the powers that had orchestrated her being invited to participate in this magical experience. "Thank you, thank you, thank you."

* * *

Madeleine woke the next day, still in the glow of the previous evening's wonder. Gifted with the most magnificent secret, she wanted to share it with the whole world, and to keep it for her very own. Life took on a new air. Her inner world felt more wondrous, her outer world more mundane. Having caught a glimpse of something real and significant, she was more keenly aware than ever of the absurdity of her menial life and the distasteful nature of her occupation.

Prior to this awakening, she had been able to compartmentalize the things she did for money and the company she was forced to keep. Now it seemed more difficult to tolerate the coarse nature of the men and women with whom she was required to share space. She wondered how Chelsea always managed to maintain such a positive outlook on life when their situations were almost identical. *How does she do it?*

The glow of the gathering gave way to the ennui of life as usual. One of the girls had noticed that she was missing the night before and felt it necessary to pry.

"Where were you last night? Off with a lover? Be a shame if the madam found out, wouldn't it?" the girl taunted.

"Oh, leave her alone. You're just jealous you have nothing better to do," another defended.

Madeleine did her best to ignore the conversation completely. Dependent on her current working situation for stability and financial security, she had no desire to rock the boat. Petty gossip wasn't worth jeopardizing her safety.

The next time she saw Chelsea, she had even more questions.

"What happened when the leader's voice changed? Why did her eyes roll back?" What did she mean about the women being divine beings?" Madeleine quizzed.

"Slow down. One at a time," Chelsea replied lightheartedly to Madeleine's rapid-fire questions. "Penelope is a channel. She was channeling an ascended master named Saint Germaine. When her eyes rolled back, it was because she was connecting to him on a higher plane, and her voice changed because he was speaking through her. His message was to our higher selves, to help us remember the truth of who we are beyond mere human form."

"So, how does all this work? How do I know that what she said is true? Do I have a higher self?" Madeleine asked.

"Yes, you absolutely have a higher self," Chelsea reassured her. "We've all forgotten our true nature as divine beings, and the first step in fulfilling our mission is to remember the truth of who we are on the spiritual plane, and then merge our human self with our higher self."

"But how do I do that?" Madeleine asked.

"A good start is to meditate and set an intention to connect with your higher self and tune into your inner wisdom. You can meditate by talking walks in nature or sitting quietly and listening. However you do it is perfect for you," Chelsea explained.

Madeleine listened, trying to understand the deeper meaning of what Chelsea was saying. She finally asked her the question that had been plaguing her for days. "How do you seem so happy and positive doing what we do and living how we live when it all seems so awful?"

Hearing the legitimate pain in her voice, Chelsea knew she must be careful and deliberate with her reply. "When you begin to tune in to the real world and the real you, the importance of this world begins to fade. You stop looking for satisfaction and significance in what's happening around you and look for true meaning and validation from within yourself. The more fully you are able to do that, the less what happens here matters, whether good or bad."

Chelsea continued. "This life is like a dream where we can learn, grow and evolve as souls but it's easy to get so caught up in desire or suffering that we forget our real purpose for coming here. In a way, hardships are catalyst to motivate us to wake up."

Penelope had channeled that to seek the respect of lost souls in a lost world was futile. To pursue privilege or position was shortsighted and foolish. Money and status were the trappings of a temporary and fallen world. Those who were drawn in and distracted by them or caught up in the emotions of ambition, jealousy, or fear failed the true test of life. They were doomed to return to this world, to try once again to learn the lessons their soul had originally come here for.

"When you can truly integrate this wisdom, you'll find peace knowing that you're achieving something beautiful and important on a soul level," Chelsea finished.

Madeleine listened. She would not be able to integrate it all right away. It would take time for her to work through her resentments and un-forgiveness in order to come into the peace that Chelsea spoke of. She didn't have a firm grasp on what Chelsea meant by a fallen world, or having to return, or the other plane of existence. It was as though Chelsea were speaking another language, and Madeleine only caught every third or fourth word. She nodded in agreement because she felt the truth of it, even though she couldn't articulate a coherent response.

Chelsea hugged her and reassured her once again that she was doing perfectly, and that, in time, she would come to understand with greater clarity.

"You've been called because you carry the light inside of you, and you're ready to remember," Chelsea told her. "You'd be miserable if you tried to walk away from your destiny now."

Madeleine knew it was true. Once you knew, you can never un-know. And life would never be the same.

Chapter 19

Shattered

The call came in the wee hours, that time of night when no one called unless it was an emergency. Sophie knew something was wrong. The news dropped her to her knees in a wail of shock and disbelief. "Nana! No, no, no...." she cried.

It was her dad on the other end. He had known she wouldn't take it well, but he didn't expect Sophie's reaction to be so intense. He had never had the deep connection with his mother that Sophie and she had shared. Theirs was a special and sacred bond only possible when two spiritually connected souls met on this earthly plane.

Caleb couldn't fully grasp the depth of their connection or the impact this news had on his daughter. Her Nana had given shape and solidity to her world. She had provided the underpinning upon which life made sense. Without her, Sophie was a ship lost at sea without an anchor, tossed about by the waves, drifting aimlessly. It felt like the very foundation of her world was shattered.

Her dad tried to comfort her as best he could, but he had never been very good at handling these types of situations. He fumbled a few words of reassurance, mostly standing dumbly on the other end of the line. When Sophie's sobs quieted, he proceeded with the details of the arrangements. Daisy had preplanned everything, so as not to be a burden on anyone when the time came. The funeral would be this coming Sunday at the Davis funeral home, twelve noon. He offered to pay for her plane fare.

"You don't need to do that, Dad. I'll be there."

Sophie wrote down the details, her mind too numb to rely on her memory. She stood for a long time after she hung up the phone. There was a ringing in her ears. Every move, even to turn her head, felt like it was in slow motion. Like a phantom, half there and half not, her legs moved towards the couch. She sat down and stared blankly at the television.

Her body vibrating, she curled up in the fetal position. She felt a burning sensation all over, as though a furnace had turned up her internal thermostat. It occurred to her that it was burning away some of the grief and shock, helping to mitigate the overwhelming emotion. She found it interesting in a detached sort of way. She had never experienced this burning sensation before, but then she had never experienced this kind of grief before. She surrendered to it.

When she was able to move again, she found her phone and called her boss to let him know she would be taking bereavement leave. She was in the middle of an important case with a court date coming up. The day before, it would have been inconceivable for her to abandon the case at such a crucial juncture. The day before, nothing had seemed more important than her success and career. Now all of that seemed insignificant. The fragility of life had stunned her into an alternate reality. All she could think of was Nana.

As the shock subsided, feelings of grief, guilt, and regret began to surface. *I should have gone to see her. I should have told her I love her.* If only she could get some of that time back.

Tears streamed down her face—tears that would not stop for weeks to come, tears that were not a petition for sympathy or comfort, tears that were for herself alone. She cried for her Nana, knowing she would never feel her gentle touch or hear her melodic voice ever again. She cried tears of loneliness and emptiness and pure loss. There were no words for this kind of sorrow.

She went through the motions that life required. She booked a plane ticket. She packed some clothes and toiletries. She made some toast and coffee. She flipped through television channels and watched the screen while her mind was miles away. She set her alarm and went to bed in time to make her flight the next day.

Her face was stone as she climbed into the Uber, walked into the airport, went through security, and sat at the gate. She had lost the ability to smile, make eye contact, or engage in even the most superficial manner. Like a robot, she placed her bag on the conveyer belt and removed her shoes without her usual thoughts of why she hadn't signed up for TSA pre-check.

Her dad picked her up from the airport. The tears began again as soon as she saw him. They swapped habitual and mindless pleasantries, him asking about her flight, her asking about his drive. He put her suitcases in the car. They rode in silence.

They were staying at the house. Nana's presence was all around. It was bittersweet to be in this place where Sophie had shared some of the happiest memories of her life, in stark contrast with the sadness that now hung in the air. Daisy's essence was a sweet perfume of joy and love, a balm for the wounded soul. Now her light had been snuffed out, abruptly and without warning. An existential crisis loomed in the shadows of Sophie's psyche. *Why does God let good people die?*

Plans had already been made for dinners and brunches in the days leading up to the services. Family had come in to pay their last respects. As they sat around the table, many shared stories about Daisy, both endearing and funny. It was good to remember her this way, to celebrate the good she had brought to the lives of so many. Sophie listened, but kept silent. What she had shared with Nana was sacred. They would never be able to understand the special, otherworldly bond they'd had. It felt like trying to explain it would tarnish it somehow.

She found herself smiling and even laughing at the tales they told. It was all so familiar. It felt so right to be together, but so wrong that Nana wasn't here to share it. Her mind wandered to Wendy. She became acutely aware that this was a kindred spirit she did not want to let slip away. *I'm definitely going to make plans to go see her as soon as I get home.*

The next few days were a whirlwind of arrangements and details, from flowers to catering. There was so much to consider. She stood after the service was over, greeting the guests one by one. Nobody really knew what to say. By the end, she thought that if one more person said, "I'm so sorry for your loss," she might scream. But what else could they say in the face of inconsolable grief? She just had to get through it.

During the few minutes she had alone, Sophie looked through her grandmother's things. She touched each knickknack and keepsake with reverence, remembering the stories Nana had told her about each one. Memories flooded her mind of the two of them sitting at the kitchen table, making cookies, playing cards, doing puzzles, memories filled with love and laughter and tenderness. Sophie felt a deep sense of gratitude. Daisy had given her so much love—love that had carried her through some of the darkest moments of her life. She had instilled a faith in her that there was yet some goodness in this world. *Thank you, Nana. I love you forever and ever.*

Sophie and her dad rode in silence back to the airport. He helped her with her bags and gave her a brief hug.

"Text me when you land," Caleb said.

"Of course," She replied.

She was on her way back to the real world, back to life as usual.

She threw herself into work to distract herself from feelings that she, as of yet, had not learned to process. Going to therapy never occurred to her. Implementing the only coping mechanism she knew, she soldiered on. She walked into the office ready to immerse herself—nay, to drown herself, in cases, clients, files, and research. She forgot the promise she had made to herself to visit Wendy.

Chapter 20

Sleeping with the Enemy

Assuming they would wither and die, Sophie buried her feelings, not knowing they merely lay dormant, waiting for the right conditions to spring to life.

For Sophie, condition's name was Simon.

It wasn't so much that Sophie was drawn in by Simon's charm and commanding masculinity. It was more that she didn't have the strength, in that moment, to resist it. In many ways, he came across as a man's man, confident and sure of himself. He was comfortable taking matters into his own hands. He planned dinner dates with full details of when and where. He arranged to pick her up. It felt good, in a way, to have someone take charge and lead for a change. Sophie was tired of being so independent.

Emotionally and energetically depleted from the toll of her grandmother's death, Sophie allowed herself to be swept up in the tide of Simon's ocean. She was in an empty and vulnerable state, looking for anything or anyone to fill the void in her heart left by the loss of Nana. He liked to be in charge, and Sophie let him. She didn't have to think, and that was a relief. She was too checked out to realize she was entering dangerous waters.

In tandem with her job, Simon provided the perfect complement of busyness to adequately distract her from anything real that was going on inside of her. She was in charge in her professional life, and acquiesced to his power in her personal life. All she needed to concern herself with was what to wear and when to be ready. He took care of the rest. She made the perfect arm candy, and the prestige of her career boosted his status. This pleased him. Sophie had brains, talent, and success, but she was still objectified in every way.

He showered Sophie with attention and gifts. With the skill of a true master, he spun an intricate web of seduction. He made her feel like she mattered and that he could not live without her. It was love-bombing at its finest.

The rapid succession of traumas that had been rained down upon her had left Sophie so numb that it took months before she noticed anything was off. Initially, the shift in his attitude was barely perceptible. His compliments began to include subtle suggestions of what she could do to improve. He disguised his insults as concern about what others might think. Increasingly, he began to point out her flaws and make her question herself in a thousand little ways.

He had successfully turned the tables. Instead of feeling like he couldn't live without her, she began to feel that she couldn't live without him. He began to imply, then state overtly, that she would never find anyone to love her besides him, that she would be lost and alone if she did anything to cause him to leave, that she was essentially flawed and unlovable. His brainwashing campaign worked. He got inside her head and completely rearranged her self-concept from a beautiful, successful, independent woman to a homely, inadequate, dependent parasite that he could barely tolerate. He had downloaded a Trojan horse virus into her mind that twisted around itself, slowly consuming her sense of self. She was gutted, dying slowly from the inside out.

Thus began a several-year stint of becoming a shell of a person, reduced to being an extension of Simon, seeing herself as only as valuable as he made her feel in the moment. Her emotions were pulled this way, then that. He would keep her on the line, neither reeling her in nor letting her go. She would be held in a ghost world of being his plaything and nothing more. She would never be free as long as it served him.

Sophie's world got smaller and smaller and smaller. She and Simon still made public appearances. He loved that her beauty and success made him look good. Of course, she had to be careful not to outshine him in any way, always deferring to his superior intelligence and success and saying how lucky she was to have him. In public, he always complimented her on how beautiful and smart she was, but on the way home, he always flipped the script. Whether it was because she was too charming or too quiet, too voluptuous or too Victorian, too pompous or too humble, he always found a way to degrade her, his resentment seething just beneath the surface.

She constantly walked on eggshells, learning to read his body language, facial expressions and moods to determine how she should act at any given moment. Life had become a game of survival, where the rules were constantly changing. It was impossible to be perfect enough to placate Simon's emotional volatility or to fill his insatiable thirst for validation. Her nervous system was in a partial state of fight or flight at all times, with occasional swings into full red-alert status. She had forgotten how to relax or feel calm. Anxiety was her constant companion.

From an early age, Sophie had learned to hide what was going on. In spite of the intolerable pressure she was under, her performance didn't slip one iota. What did change was her ability to enjoy her success or to give herself credit for her wins. She had shifted from being proud of her talents to nervously trying to prove that she was good enough. She began to approach each case with a fear that she might fail or get it wrong. She was losing herself.

Simon's thoughts became her thoughts, and his way of doing things became hers. She was living his life, serving only to please him in exchange for crumbs of attention. It was pitiful and sickening to watch, which was why she hid from everyone. She always found an excuse to bow out of invitations where concerned and caring friends might get a glimpse of her sadness, or where, in the presence of genuine compassion, her vulnerability might surface.

She continued to engage in social events when Simon demanded it. Those engagements were different. She would put on her mask and act the part. In those situations, it was as if she were directing her avatar to go through the motions while she remained disengaged and dissociated.

Simon fit the profile of a classic narcissist. Sophie was his supply. Having grown up with a narcissistic mother, he had been ruthlessly shamed for every aspect of self-expression until every shred of authenticity was stripped from him. His true self was completely obliterated. There was nothing behind the mask. He was empty inside, a black hole that demanded to be filled with the life force energy and light of others.

At rare moments, Simon showed his vulnerability and emptiness. It was brief and usually followed by compensatory anger and defensiveness. Because of the rejection and shame he had received in response to any sensitivity as a child, he had developed a hatred for weakness in himself and others. These moments always pulled on Sophie's heartstrings, stirring feelings of compassion and renewing her hope that her love would be enough nurture him back to wholeness.

She was wrong.

Weeks rolled into months rolled into years. Simon continued to dominate and manipulate her. He routinely pushed her this way, pulled her that way, and withdrew his love and attention as ploys to trigger her emotions and extract her life force energy on which he fed. He had turned her into a pauper, pleading with him to love her, crying for him to acknowledge her feelings, begging him not to leave.

In the situation with Alex, her higher self worked through circumstances to steer her back onto her path. This time, it was the still, small voice of her wounded inner child that finally pierced through the din to gain her attention. Simon was never going to leave her. He would hold her in no-man's-land, always threatening to abandon her while never letting her move on and heal.

On a Tuesday afternoon, when nothing in particular was going on, something inside of Sophie broke. Seemingly out of nowhere, an awareness bubbled up that she could not continue living this way. The voice inside of her, which she had hushed for so long, insisted that she remember who she was.

Experience had taught her that trying to talk to Simon about it would only open the door to more mind games and manipulation. She knew she could not give him that opportunity. She had been duped for the last time.

He was away on one of his infamous business trips. She had long suspected he was having an affair. Whenever she had confronted him with the inconsistencies of his actions and cover stories, he had gaslighted her with accusations that she was jealous and delusional. That day, she realized that she no longer cared. She could no longer conjure the energy to vie for his attention or to save their relationship.

She packed her clothes, toiletries, and a few personal items. It wasn't worth the argument that would ensue if she tried to take any household items, whether she had purchased them or not. The stuff didn't matter. She could replace it. She would start fresh. Peace was her only priority.

She found a fully furnished short-term rental near her job. There was no need for a moving truck. She loaded the few things she would be taking with her into her car, shook the dust off her feet, and drove away.

For the first time in her life, Sophie decided she needed therapy. Thus far, she had bumbled her way through life, blindly banging her head against the walls. It was a clumsy and crude means of staying on course. She could no longer ignore the obvious: her inner compass had failed her. She was head smart and successful, but when it came to matters of the heart, she was lost.

When Simon returned to find she had vacated their high-rise apartment, he was livid. His ego would not and could not accept that she had taken a stand and stepped into her power. He pulled out all the stops. He called and texted her incessantly. He made threats. He sent flowers to her office. He showed up unannounced at her workplace. It wasn't because he loved her that he fought so hard to win her back. It was because by leaving, she had deprived him of his narcissistic supply. But the kitchen was closed.

It took months before he finally stopped stalking her. Eventually, he found a suitable replacement and transferred his efforts onto his new target. In spite of that, he was never really okay with letting Sophie go. Months and even years after their split, he would leave her taunting text messages and voicemails oscillating between rage and flattery. His insatiable need could never be satisfied with a single source. Whenever his tank was low, he would seek out people from his past for a dopamine hit. He couldn't bear the feelings of shame that began to surface whenever outside validation deserted him. He hated being alone. More specifically, he hated himself when he was alone.

Sophie had to remind herself that it wasn't her problem. He was an adult. He was capable of seeking help if he so chose. She could only make the right choice for one person. It was time to think of herself.

Chapter 21

Just What the Doctor Ordered

Sophie had physically divorced herself from Simon, but it would take much longer to extricate him from her mind. Once set in motion, the program of self-doubt continued to run and create havoc in her life. She had taken on his criticisms as her own. His voice was inside of her head, constantly reminding her of her shortcomings and failures. Even though he had pushed her past her limits, she still wrestled with guilt and often blamed herself for the failure of the relationship. She wondered if, after all, it was her fault, as he had told her so many times. *Maybe I was too demanding. Was I just thinking of myself? Maybe I'm the narcissist.*

These and many more questions rattled around her brain. Her therapist, Victoria, did a great job of helping her put things in perspective and see Simon for what he was. She explained that he was manipulative, emotionally abusive, and self serving. She contended that he would likely never change, and in reality, could never change.

During their sessions, Sophie would outwardly agree, but inside, she didn't buy it. Her therapist educated her on the stages of narcissistic abuse: idealization, devaluing, discarding, and finally hoovering at which point they sucked their victim back into the cycle all over again. Sophie could see how Simon had cycled through this pattern repeatedly over their years together. She knew that what Victoria told her made logical sense, but she couldn't integrate it in the places where it really mattered. She knew it was true, but she couldn't feel it. It seemed that nothing short of an exorcism would remove him from her soul.

The greatest injury she had suffered was her inability to trust herself. Her psyche was fractured. She was emotionally conflicted and anxious. Some aspects of her were capable and strong ,while others were traumatized and weak. As she continued her journey of introspection and self-reflection, Victoria helped her see that her life had been a succession of traumas. Considering everything she had been through, she had coped very well, but it had taken a toll.

To face one's shadow is not for the faint of heart. To heal the secret, empty places inside of her, which had been hiding for so long, was a daunting task. To finally feel the feelings she had tried so desperately to avoid required a kind of courage that few possess.

She tookVictoria's advice to show herself grace. It wasn't something Sophie was used to. Her compulsive need to be productive in order to feel validated was a hard habit to break. She started to take a few moments, here and there, to just be. She took walks in the park, giving herself permission to leave her phone at home. Quieting her mind seemed impossible, but she tried meditating anyway. At first, she could barely sit still for five minutes, but as she began to develop a daily practice, she found she adjusted to longer and longer periods of stillness. She took a yoga class. She became more in tune with her body, and noticed as she did that her emotions began to flow more freely. She was finding herself, getting to know herself ,and even beginning to like herself.

It was then that she remembered the promise she had made to herself to visit Wendy. The mere thought of it felt like an ocean breeze on a warm, sunny day. Yes, she would go see Wendy and take an actual vacation, something she had not done since she started at the firm.

Wendy was excited to hear from her.

"Yes, yes, yes!" she exclaimed in response to Sophie's request. She had extended an open invitation years ago, but Sophie had never taken her up on it. They discussed some dates that worked for both of them. Wendy wanted to make sure she had time off work, so they could spend quality time together.

Knowing she had something to look forward to brightened Sophie's spirits. She just needed to get through the next couple of weeks, and she would be lying on the beach in sunny California.

* * *

Wendy met her at the airport, waving wildly and grinning from ear to ear. They had met at a time in their lives when life was still fresh and optimistic. They were free to be, do, or go wherever they wanted. They were at their best in those years.

Being in Wendy's energy field brought out the best in Sophie. She had always had that effect on her. She was transported back to the early days of university, before Alex, before Nana had died, before Simon. Wendy held space for Sophie to get in touch with herself again, more vividly than she had been able to with walks or yoga. Sophie had stepped into a different paradigm, and it was wonderful.

They stayed up late into the night, talking about boys and jobs and bosses and family. Sophie told her about Nana passing.

"Why didn't you call me?" Wendy asked.

"I don't know. I wanted to, but it was just too hard to talk about. I actually wanted to come see you, but you know how it is. Life." Sophie shrugged her shoulders and shook her head.

Wendy told her about a new aspect of herself that she was exploring. Her spiritual side, she called it. She had always felt like there was more to life than meets the eye. There had been a stirring inside of her ,like her soul was calling her to wake up and discover the truth of who she was.

"I know it sounds strange," Wendy said.

"Not at all, weirdo," Sophie teased. "You know I think you're the bee's knees, Wendy, so if you're into it, there must be something to it," She reassured her.

"Thank you, Sophie. That really means a lot to me." Wendy continued, "I won't overwhelm you with my full crazy all at once, but I'd love to tell you about a couple of amazing experiences I've had sometime."

"Deal," Sophie replied, yawning.

They passed out, both feeling as if they were home.

The next morning, they went to the beach. Sophie couldn't recall the last time she had been to the ocean. Her dad and grandparents had taken her once when she was twelve. Then there was the trip to Cancun she had taken with Simon and his work colleagues. It would have been great, except for one thing: he was there. It had been impossible to relax or enjoy it. She was always walking on eggshells whenever he was around, and vacation was no exception. He wanted to make sure, to his friends, that it looked like she was having a good time, while behind the scenes, he worked hard to make sure she didn't. *That beach trip didn't even count.*

She had never once taken a vacation with her mother. Ohio, where she had grown up, was not exactly the adventure capital of the world. Even if it had been, Justine could never plan beyond the next couple of days. She was in constant survival mode, always coping with the latest self-imposed crisis.

Sophie's dad and Nana always made sure she got the most out of her time with them. They took her to the drive-in movies and water park every year. Their trip to the beach was an extra-special affair. She rode the rides on the boardwalk, swam in the ocean, and built sand castles. It was hands down the most memorable vacation they had taken together.

As Sophie reflected on the scant list of holidays in her life, she realized she was rather vacation-deprived. She couldn't remember her grandparents on her mother's side ever indulging in activities for pure pleasure. Fun and adventure weren't part of their family culture. They were stern and serious people. A brief insight into her mother's childhood flashed across her awareness. For the first time, she felt a little sorry for her.

Here she was in glorious California on one of its glorious beaches. It was fabulous. She looked amazing with her new yoga body. She wore a big-brimmed sun hat and stylish sun glasses. She could have been a model. She had smiled briefly as she glanced at herself in the mirror on the way out the door. *Not too shabby, Miss Davenport.*

Lying here, feeling the warmth of the sun, hearing the ocean waves, and seeing children playing, she lost all sense of herself as a separate being, merging with the joy of life expressing all around her. She took a deep breath and let it out with a sigh. *Thank you, thank you, thank you.* Her expression of gratitude wasn't directed at anyone in particular. Sophie had never been religious, and as of yet, had not explored her spiritual side, but lying here now, she definitely felt a connection with something greater than herself. It was great, and it was good. She felt the same goodness she had felt with Nana. A smile broke across her face.

"What are you grinning about?" Wendy poked.

"Nothing and everything," Sophie replied.

Wendy looked her in the eyes and nodded. She knew what she meant. She was so glad Sophie had come. She secretly hoped Sophie would find the healing she needed here. She hoped but she had no agenda. She had no need to be anyone's rescuer or savior; she had transcended that paradigm. She understood that it was enough to be in the energy of love and grace. She knew that holding space allowed others to transform in her presence—that and the sun and the ocean, of course.

Just being here was definitely a good start. Sophie hadn't realized how much she needed to connect to the earth and nature. Certainly, Chicago was fabulous in its own right. The buildings were an architectural feat, and the hustle and bustle of the city had an excitement to it. In many ways, she had been enamored with it. Being surrounded by professionals and financial institutions felt like being on the cutting edge, the center of what was happening in the world. It was easy to get caught up in its grandiosity. But lying on the beach was a total pattern break. She was able to think more clearly and remember that there was more to life than career and status and being impressive. Watching the seagulls swoop and dive and seeing the sand crabs burrow in the sand put her ambition and self-image in perspective. There was a peace in feeling smaller while a part of something so much bigger.

Sophie drank in all that life offered her that day. She melted into the earth. It was a meditative experience, and she dissolved into the all. Spirit flowed into, through, and all around her. With each breath, she felt as if Spirit was breathing her, infusing life force energy into all levels of her being, filling the empty, contracted places inside of her. *I could lie here forever.*

Not until the sun was setting did they pack up and leave. They were both starving, so they stopped in at a restaurant overlooking the ocean for one last goodbye. Wave-tossed and sun-drenched, food had never tasted better. She savored the flavors and textures, being fully present to their deliciousness. *Everyone deserves one perfect day in their lifetime. This is mine.*

Wendy had planned a few events while Sophie was there, making sure there was plenty of downtime in between. When the time felt right, Wendy opened up about some of her personal journey of spirituality. She had taken a deep dive into shadow work to clear out her old childhood wounds and traumas. While the process was intense, the results were amazing. She explained how it had freed her from self-doubt and anxiety. She had shifted patterns that had kept her stuck in a cycle of less-than-satisfying relationships and self-sabotage. Sophie was surprised and a little shocked to hear this; Wendy had always been the healthiest and happiest person she knew. It was hard to imagine that she needed to heal or change anything.

Wendy had so much to share that it was hard to unpack it all. What resonated with Sophie the most was her enthusiasm and gratitude.

"It's changed my life so much, Sophie. Everyone deserves to feel this good. It feels like my mission to help others the same way I've been helped," she shared.

"When you say you're making it your mission to help others, do you mean professionally?" Sophie inquired.

"I haven't quit my day job just yet." Wendy laughed. "But I am thinking about it. For now, I'm doing free sessions and perfecting my skills," she added.

"Wow, that's a big jump from law," Sophie commented.

"I know. I get that it doesn't make logical sense, but when you find something you're truly passionate about, it feels like a calling."

Sophie listened, but didn't respond. Wendy was right: it didn't make logical sense. They had both spent years and a ton of money becoming attorneys. It seemed a little crazy to just walk away from all that. It certainly didn't make financial sense.

"The thing is, this work changed my life—I mean, *really* changed it. I could never put into words how transformational it's been. What I can tell you is that my relationships have become so much richer and more connected. I feel a deep sense of satisfaction with my life, and a deep, indescribable peace inside," Wendy went on.

That definitely caught Sophie's attention. *Wow. Peace and satisfaction.* She was a little jealous of what Wendy had. Sophie was beginning to find more stability, but she still wrestled with the aftermath of her relationship with Simon. What Wendy was describing felt a long ways away. Sophie had been focused on getting back to who she had been before she was taken over by Simon. After listening to Wendy, she was beginning to realize that returning to the status quo might not be such a great aspiration after all. Wendy was opening her eyes to the potential for so much more.

"Maybe you can try a session while you're here," Wendy offered.

Sophie felt an irrational fear well up in her chest. She had no idea why, but it felt terrifying. It was as if some part of her knew there were things she might have to face that she had worked very hard to compartmentalize and suppress. The prospect of dredging up old feelings was terrifying.

"I'll think about it," she responded.

Wendy didn't push. She understood how the subconscious mind works. She understood how hidden parts of us keep trying to protect us in old, worn-out ways that don't really work but give us a semblance of control.

She went on to tell her about her new beau, Jeff. She had always managed to have drama free relationships with men, but she had never found true intimacy until now. She fully attributed this change to the inner work she had done. She had faced a hidden fear of commitment, which had emerged in childhood as a result of a workaholic father. There was no conflict to speak of between her parents, so she had never taken on the more noticeable dysfunctional patterns of arguing and fighting. Her dad just wasn't around much. Her parents' relationship was stable and reliable, drama-free. Everyone was pleasant, yet she never witnessed any affection or genuine intimacy. This surface-level connection was what she knew and what she had replicated in her adult romantic relationships.

She hadn't been aware of how unsatisfying it was until she started paying attention to her pattern of relationships that never went anywhere. They were pleasant and fun, but lacked any real intimacy or commitment. Usually, the men left. She had always seen herself as emotionally stable and independent, so she dismissed it as a character flaw in them. But when she had fallen in love with her former partner, Manny, the old story she had told herself so many times no longer consoled her. For the first time, she wanted more, and she really wanted it to work—and for the first time, she had to admit that she didn't know how to make that happen.

"Pain is our greatest teacher," Wendy's hypnotherapist had told her. "We don't have to learn the hard way, but we're not usually motivated to change when everything is peaches and cream."

Manny was the first man Wendy had truly fallen in love with. He was open and authentic and emotionally connected. She wanted to give her heart to him. The problem was, she didn't know how to be vulnerable or transparent. Manny had grown up in a household with emotional intimacy and tons of affection. His relationship with Wendy felt one-dimensional, like she was behind a glass wall. It wasn't the deep connection he was looking for.

When he tried to explain his feelings, Wendy, quite literally, didn't know what he was talking about. She had no reference for what he was trying to convey. She weakly tried to blame him for being too demanding, but, inside, she was afraid there might be some truth to what he was saying. Because of her inability to discuss his needs in a constructive way, their conversations went in circles without ever being resolved. It was clear that nothing was going to change.

To his credit, Manny refused to settle. He wasn't angry with Wendy, and he didn't blame her. He just knew what he wanted, knew what he deserved ,and had enough self esteem and self care to be true to himself. He had walked away.

Wendy was crushed, and she was confused. She could no longer see herself as superior, above people who let their messy emotions ruin their lives. Her avoidance of authentic emotions was not the solution she had assumed it to be. Her self-protective mechanisms had become her demise. She found herself spinning out of control in a way she had often pitied in others. She couldn't fix this. She needed help.

She'd started going to a therapist that a friend of hers recommended. It helped to know that she wasn't crazy or irreparably broken. She was able to talk through feelings that were coming up that she had never dealt with before. She had never recognized that she had experienced many childhood mini-traumas, the kind that seemed like no big deal, but which had wounded her tender heart. There were countless times where her feelings had been discounted or ignored. There were so many times she had felt unseen and unheard.

Wendy developed a complex system of coping mechanisms where she appeared to be well adjusted and emotionally intelligent. However, if a situation arose where true vulnerability was required, she preemptively shut it down, steering clear of uncomfortable emotions. From her perspective, it worked magnificently. She had a series of fun, engaging, sexy relationships where guys would invariably fall in love with her. But the moment they wanted something deeper or more real, she bolted. She had a classic avoidant attachment style and had left a trail of casualties in her wake while barely batting an eye. When Manny left, it had been her wake-up call.

Therapy helped, but Wendy had begun to feel like she was hitting a brick wall. She gained a great deal of awareness about her issues and where they had originated, but it wasn't enough to change her unconscious programs. In some ways, it was almost more frustrating to understand the problem, but still feel powerless to change it. She was circling the heart of the matter, but could never quite get to it.

Wendy decided to look for outside-the-box solutions. She started by going to a nearby psychic shop, mostly out of curiosity. She looked through their crystal selection and chose a few that promised to help with various emotions and blockages. They were beautiful, anyway. It couldn't hurt. She also got a tarot reading. She knew it was silly to put stock in something so superstitious, but she was surprised at how insightful the woman was. The psychic knew specific details about her past relationships and about the heartbreak Wendy was going through. She gave her some advice about what she could do to improve things moving forward.

In spite of her skepticism, Wendy became intrigued with the paranormal and psychic phenomena. Prior to this, she had seen it as juvenile, putting it in the category of parlor tricks or street magic. Now she felt like there was something more to it, something real. She felt irresistibly drawn to the metaphysical, as if her soul were calling to her.

Wendy learned about chakras, life force energy called Qi and how to remove energetic blockages. She attended sound bowl ceremonies and took a Reiki class. She could really feel the energy running through her body, like an aspect of her being was coming back online.

A friend of hers told her about her experience with hypnotherapy and that she had achieved, in one or two sessions, what may have taken years with traditional therapy. It was a compelling testimonial. Wendy started researching hypnosis and hypnotherapy to learn what it was all about. She felt both a strong desire and a deep-seated resistance. It was as though she had a tug-of-war going on inside of her. It took weeks for her to finally pull the trigger and schedule an appointment.

Sarah was very welcoming and put her at ease right away. She had a way of knowing the right questions to ask to get to the heart of the matter. She explained, in an easy-to-understand way, the difference between the conscious mind and the subconscious mind. She broke down how so much of what drives our behavior is completely outside of our conscious awareness. The subconscious is driving the boat, and we're just along for the ride.

"That's why people can be so smart and still be a little crazy," Sarah joked.

"It does feel that way a lot of the time," Wendy acknowledged.

Mostly, Sarah was a really great listener. She lovingly and tenaciously drew forth the answers to questions that Wendy had never considered asking herself before. She had numerous light bulb moments in their short conversation. She helped her identify a few key memories where her patterns of emotional detachment had begun.

Sarah had a very unique approach to resolving trauma and rewiring patterns in the subconscious. Her techniques were powerful without being forceful. Like a lever with a perfectly positioned fulcrum, she had a finesse that allowed her to create dramatic results with the smallest effort. It was as elegant as it was transformative.

After identifying some of the key elements to Wendy's emotionally avoidant patterns, Sarah took her into hypnosis, where they got to work. She was guided to comfort and reassure her wounded inner child. She was coached on owning her voice and confronting the people who had hurt her. She was shown the magic of giving positive emotional resources to the key players that radically transformed the energy of everyone involved. It was beautiful. It was comprehensive. It was life-changing. Wendy walked out of that room a changed person, lighter, brighter, born anew.

Wendy did her best to put into words the profound nature of her experience. Of course, words could never do it justice. Someone can tell you what it's like to skydive, but you can't possibly know until you actually experience it.

It was terrifying and exhilarating and freeing. Wendy beamed as she prattled on and on, eager to impart how life-changing it had been.

Sophie took it all in. The fear began to come up in her chest again. Wendy's account was very compelling, and she was happy for her. She could tell that it really meant something to her. But Sophie wasn't Wendy. Opening up about these kinds of things was more difficult for her. She heard what Wendy had said about memories where she had learned to shut down her feelings. Sophie didn't discount Wendy's childhood wounds. However, they paled in comparison to her own. Sophie had witnessed drama and trauma almost daily since infancy. There was going to be a lot more to dredge up and unpack, and it was going to be a lot more overwhelming.

"Let's go dancing!" she said, changing the subject.

Wendy looked at her for a long moment. She understood that it's usually the people who need this type of work the most who are the least likely to seek it out. Everyone's on their own timing.

"Let's do it!" Wendy responded enthusiastically.

They immediately went back into schoolgirl mode, trying on dresses, putting on makeup, and deciding where to go. There were several places with live music. They agreed that some place low key held more appeal than a typical nightclub. After reviewing their options, they picked a local bar in the downtown area and headed out. Their destination was in close proximity to several other venues within walking distance. It was perfect.

Vinny's was packed. Being together in this environment was reminiscent of their college days together. They were two hot mamas on the loose. Sophie stepped right back into her sexy, flirtatious persona—the one that used to come out to play after a few too many drinks. She was less inhibited than she had been in college, so she no longer needed to get tipsy to channel her inner vixen. The atmosphere, the music, and the crowd were enough to bring that part out of her. Once a synaptic pathway is forged in the brain, it's easier to reignite it.

Sophie motioned to Wendy. "Grab those two seats. I'll get us some drinks."

She floated over to the bar. Beautiful and buxom, she quickly gained the bartender's attention by leaning a bit too far over the bar.

"What can I get for you?" the bartender asked, his eyes smiling.

"Two lemon drop martinis, sir," Sophie replied.

"Two lemon drop martinis for the lady," he repeated.

She watched him as he made their drinks. *Yummy* When he turned around unexpectedly, she knew she was busted. She smiled and lifted her eyebrows in admiration. For a moment, she felt like she was channeling Wendy's bodacious younger self rather than her own. *Well, I did learn from the best.*

She walked back towards Wendy, bearing her gifts.

"Lemon drops!" Wendy exclaimed. "Just like old times."

"Yes, but now we can afford to buy our own drinks!" Sophie laughed.

They laughed and flirted and chatted with several guys. Wendy was in a relationship and her new boyfriend was perfect for her. She couldn't have imagined that she would meet someone that she could love even more than Manny, but she had. She had done the inner work and was finally capable of an intimate and authentic relationship. The universe had rewarded her by bringing Jeff into her life.

Wendy graciously checked any men who seemed a little too interested by casually bringing up Jeff in the conversation. She was there as Sophie's wingman. One particularly handsome gentleman held Sophie's attention. He knew how to carry himself. He was confident, but not cocky. He kept circling back to check on her every few minutes. He wasn't annoying or obnoxious, but he made sure she knew she was the one he had his eye on.

Sophie danced with a variety of men, but she saved the last dance for the tall, handsome man, whose name was Jackson. The band made the announcement that they would be playing their last song of the night. Before she could blink, Jackson was there. He took her by the hand and led her onto the dance floor.

She put her cheek against his as he pulled her body closer. The smell of his cologne was intoxicating. The way he moved was graceful. He took command of her body in such a way that to follow his lead was as natural as breathing. She was aroused. Before he even asked, she knew she would be going home with him that night. The magnetic attraction was palpable.

Wendy wasn't exactly surprised when Sophie informed her that she would see her in the morning rather than going home with her. She had already planned on spending the night with Jeff, so she was happy to be spared the inconvenience of giving Sophie a ride.

"Text me the address and his license plate," Wendy cautioned. Even in the passion of the moment, women had to always be cognizant of safety first.

"I will, Mama," Sophie promised with a wink.

Jackson was a Southern cowboy type with broad shoulders that narrowed to a tight waist. He said "yes ma'am" or "no ma'am" when talking and made a point of opening doors for her. There was something a little special about Southern charm that made a girl feel taken care of and safe. It was sexy and endearing.

He was the perfect combination of tenderness and take-control. She was putty in his hands, and she loved it. He studied every inch of her body, taking his time, getting to know her intimately. He made his way down from her face and neck to her waist. There he stopped, leaving her aching for more. He started again at her toes and made his way up to her hips, where he stopped once again. He enjoyed watching her writhe with longing and desire.

Jackson had mastered the art of seduction, making it both exquisite and torturous. Sophie had never felt her body respond the way it did to his touch. Her entire mind was consumed with the need to have him inside of her. She felt desperate to consummate their union.

"Please, baby. I want you," She whispered.

When he knew she could bear it no longer, he acquiesced to her pleas. She gasped as he entered her. Minutes later, she exploded in ecstasy.

"Oh my god. I needed that." Sophie laughed as she rolled over and kissed him on the cheek. "You are a god," She added. "I need this on speed dial."

"I just aim to please, ma'am," Jackson said with his unassuming charm.

"You." Sophie pointed a finger at him. "Wow… Just wow."

Jackson was just what the doctor ordered. Like shocking a pool to rapidly eliminate contaminants, her earth-shaking orgasm had exorcised the noxious energy from her system in a flash of electricity. The release left her body limp with relaxation. He brought her some iced tea. They laid in the afterglow for a few minutes. She drifted off to sleep, a content look on her face.

Life is definitely getting better.

Chapter 22 -

A Gentleman Caller

Madeleine had several gentlemen who sought out her services on a regular basis. In addition to her beauty, she had a *je ne sais quoi* quality that kept them spell bound. They were willing to wait and to pay more for her secret sauce.

One gentleman in particular could not stay away. He was married with family, facts which Madeleine was neither in a position nor had the inclination to judge. She enjoyed his company above all the rest. While there were a few she found amusing, most of the men she entertained, she could barely tolerate. Mr. Giles was different. Truth be told, she enjoyed his company so well that she would have freely given him her time. Of course, he always made sure to more than generously compensate her.

"Back so soon? " she often teased when he showed up too many days in a row.

"I'm afraid so. Pathetic, really," he played along.

"I'm not sure it's fitting to indulge such unbridled impulses, Mr. Giles," she admonished.

"Please, miss, take pity on a poor soul," he pretended to plead.

"I suppose. Just this once." She acquiesced, kissing him cheekily.

There was a special connection between them. Often, he preferred to engage her in conversation rather than indulge his sexual appetites. He felt free when he was with her. His relationship with his wife was a reflection of the suffocatingly proper and austere society of which they were a part. Every action, every word was calculated and measured. Affection, even between couples, was viewed as unseemly. There was a shadow of control that for-bade him to ever speak or move according to his true thoughts and feelings. In his world, everyone lived behind a mask, acting out an unspoken yet perfectly understood moral code, careful never to reveal their true self.

With Madeleine, it was different. He had no need for pretense, no need to carefully guard his feelings or monitor his words. He could just be. He absolutely adored her authenticity. She felt like a real person. The way she spoke and laughed and moved was the antithesis of the calculated manner-isms and responses he was constantly surrounded by in his formal life. He could feel her very essence. She was an oasis in the desert. For so long, he had thirsted for something real.

Madeleine came to life whenever he was around. What Mr. Giles did not understand was that all of the qualities he loved about her were a con-sequence of being in his presence. He brought out the best in her. She laughed because of him. She opened up and shared her hopes and dreams because of him. The way she sashayed across the room was because of him.

These were those little moments that brought out the magic of life. It was a true love affair of the heart. They lay next to each other, staring into each other's eyes, breathing in rhythm, cheek to cheek, heart to heart. His touch sent electricity through her body, ripples of energy and ecstasy that were inexplicable. She felt as if he were caressing her very soul. That was his wish: to hold her so tightly that their hearts melded wholly into one.

There are no words to explain what is happening at times like these. Humans, being limited to the awareness of their five senses, cannot perceive the energy exchange between two souls who are in sync with each other, who share a history beyond time and space. They didn't know what it was, but they felt it, and that was enough.

Madeleine was under no delusion as to the nature and limitations of their relationship. He was constrained by the expectations of his position in society and the demands of his family. That didn't stop her from fantasizing about what their life might be like if things were different. But it wasn't different. He had taken vows, and his integrity would not permit him to violate them. His life and duty belonged to his wife.

"I…" he started to say, but stopped himself.

"I know," Madeleine responded, looking into his eyes and nodding almost imperceptibly.

He knew that Madeleine knew that he loved her. He did not have to say it. He didn't want to imply any promises he could not keep. The words *I love you* carried with them a commitment that he could not fulfill. He felt it, but he did not want to hurt her by saying it. She took his hand and placed it on her heart.

Eventually, when he knew he could no longer trust himself to act with prudence or restraint, he arranged to remove himself from this compromising position. Mr. Giles and his family were to move to another town in another county, where he would no longer have to wrestle with the temptation of Madeleine.

But neither time nor distance could sever the bond between them. This unrequited yet true love would live on forever, untarnished by the stresses or disappointments of real life. The beauty of their love would be preserved forever as a perfect moment in time, pure and eternal.

He did not say goodbye. He knew he wouldn't have the resolve to follow through if he had to look her in the eye. He sent a letter instead. She wanted to hate him for it, but she knew it was better this way. The pain of his absence was excruciating. She would have gladly crawled across broken glass if, at the other end, he would be there waiting for her. She had never known heartbreak before. She held the letter to her lips and wept.

Chapter 23

Never Alone

The full moon was approaching. Madeleine made arrangements, as she usually did, for one of the other girls to watch Steffan.

"Going out again this Friday, are ye? And where are you off to this time?" Peggy quizzed.

Peggy was a girl of average looks whose primary pleasure in life was being a busybody. She had no real interests of her own, so she fed on gossip and getting in the middle of other people's business. Madeleine was annoyed and wanted to say something sarcastic. She knew, however, that she had better be careful. Peggy was small-minded and petty enough to rat her out to win favor with the madam of the house. Madeleine's mouth and nose wrinkled in an involuntary expression of disgust. She remembered something funny one of the groomsmen had said when she had still been a servant in Master Wilson's house. *"It could be that the purpose of your life is to serve as a warning to others."* She smiled inwardly, happy, at least, that she was nothing like Peggy.

"Never you mind," Madeleine replied to Peggy.

"You're up to no good, then, are ya?" Peggy goaded.

"Ah, Peggy. I do wish you had something better to worry your pretty little head about. I would have invited you, but I don't think you'd be interested. Any time you have a personal engagement, I'd be happy to cover for you," Madeleine pivoted and redirected.

"Maybe I will come with you sometime, Maddy girl, maybe I will. Of course, I can't come this Friday, as I have a date with Mr. Pinkerton," Peggy maneuvered in kind.

"I shall look forward to it." Madeleine held her cards close to her chest. They both knew she would never extend an invitation for Peggy to join her.

The days passed quickly. At nightfall on the appointed day, Madeleine slipped out of the brothel unnoticed. She had become comfortable with this routine of getting everything in order. She was still careful, but perhaps less vigilant than she had once been. What had slipped her attention was a woman waiting for her, unseen, in the shadows of a dark alley. Madeleine made it out the door without incident. She assumed she was in the clear.

She was particularly excited about tonight. Penelope was going to be doing psychic and mediumship readings. Madeleine had never experienced this before. She was curious, for obvious reasons. On a personal note, she wished with every part of her being that her mother would appear or have a message for her. She had died so long ago now, but Madeleine still thought about her every single day.

Madeleine half walked, half ran to the circle in the woods. Not once did she suspect that she was being followed. Everyone greeted her warmly when she arrived. In addition to the messages that were to be delivered that night, Chelsea was going to be initiated into the order of Divine Sibyls. She had been training for a couple of years and had developed her gift of divination. Her predictions and psychic abilities had proven very reliable, and the head of the coven had decided she was ready. Chelsea was beside herself with excitement, but tried to maintain an air of formality.

When Penelope joined the circle, she stood silently, waiting for the others to notice. Their voices quickly fell as they became aware of her presence. First, she would handle the business of initiating Chelsea. She gave a short speech acknowledging Chelsea's many accomplishments, her dedication and natural talent. Madeleine felt so proud of her dear friend and knew that no one was more deserving. Chelsea's best attribute was her pure and precious heart. She was kind and unjaded, in spite of the considerable trials life had thrown her way. She was a rare gem, radiating her love and beauty with a brilliance that melted the hearts of all who were privileged to know her. Madeleine looked at her with awe.

Once the initiation was complete, each woman came and stood in front of Chelsea one by one. With hands folded together in front of their heart, each bowed their head, saying, *"Namaste."* Chelsea glowed with pride and gratitude.

Everyone settled back into the circle. Silence fell once again upon the group. Penelope stood tall and erect. Her eyes scanned the women before her, stopping on Madeleine.

"Step forward," Penelope invited.

Madeleine did so, feeling both nervous and eager. Penelope closed her eyes and put herself in a light trance to connect with Spirit. The words that came next were not her own, but channeled from a light being beyond this world.

"Madeleine," she began, "you are one of us. You are a being of light on a mission to assist your fellow men and women in their awakening, to assist them in remembering the truth of who they are as divine beings. You are on your path and moving in the right direction. We see you. We acknowledge you. We are with you."

Penelope took a deep breath. She paused for a full minute before continuing. "I see a woman. She has a message for you. She says, "I love you. I'm sorry I had to leave you. I'm always watching over you. You are never alone."

Tears came to Madeleine's eyes. She could feel her mother's presence and knew these were her words. She choked up with tears of intense emotion, a mixture of love, loss, and gratitude. *I love you, Mama. Thank you, thank you, thank you.*

She carried these gifts in her heart. Life had taken on a magical quality. She was connected to something real, yet mystical—something that made the best and the worst of this world seem dull and insignificant. Without even knowing it, she was beginning to embody nonattachment and nonresistance. The Buddha would have been proud.

Chapter 24

Blasphemy

Life could not have prepared her for what was to come next. They stormed into her room, snatching her out of bed and throwing her on the floor. Steffan, now crying, was taken from her arms and removed from the room. Madeleine lay stunned and speechless as accusations and questions were thrust upon her.

"Where did you go last night? Who were you with? What did you do there? Are you a witch?" A man, dressed in all black, shouted.

"What?!" was all Madeleine could muster. In her half-asleep state, she was confused about what was happening.

As if slapped across the face, she woke up and gathered her wits. "Where is my son? Bring him to me!" she demanded.

"We will not," the man in black boomed. "We will not now or ever give a child over to a witch and a whore."

"A *witch*?" Madeleine responded, genuinely perplexed. "No, no!" she defended. "I'm a simple woman, but a good mother. Please, sir, bring him back for the sake of the child!"

"You will make no demands, woman, nor requests. That is my job," he taunted.

"Please, sir, tell me, what causes you to say these things? What is it that I have done?" Madeleine pleaded.

"You have been identified as one attending a gathering of witches, communing with the devil and casting spells," he declared.

"Who told you this?" Madeleine wondered.

He pointed to Peggy.

"She was with them witches! I saw her myself, sir," Peggy fawned smugly.

Madeleine felt the blood drain out of her face. She now understood what was happening and the seriousness of the situation. She understood that Peggy, insipid and sadistic, had jumped at the chance to promote herself at Madeleine's expense. She would have sold her own mother for a bit of attention.

Madeleine knew she could not convincingly deny Peggy's accusations. It was obvious that Peggy had followed her and reported to these men everything she had witnessed. Madeleine was not only struck with fear for her personal safety, she was terrified for what would happen to the other women in the group. Their sacred fellowship had been violated—and she was to blame. She felt sick to her stomach with guilt and regret. With an icy stare, she looked Peggy in the eye. *I hate you.*

The men grabbed her and forced her to walk with them. She was to be held in jail to await trial for her crimes. She would be interrogated about the goings-on of the gathering and the identities of the other participants. There were no words to express her horror. In a single moment, she had been betrayed, lost her son, accused of an impossible-to-defend-against crime, taken to jail, and burdened with the guilt of implicating the women she cherished and cared for most.

Goaded by her accusers, she followed wide-eyed and dumb to her predetermined fate. Every now and then, one of the men would shove her to reiterate his dominance. People on the street stared and pointed as they marched along. These types of events were a delicious distraction from their repetitive, boring lives. They gathered to gossip and speculate as to what Madeleine's crime could be. She saw no compassion in the faces of the onlookers. She knew they gave no consideration to her possible innocence. Like piranhas, they fed on the misfortune of others to make themselves feel better about their own miserable existence.

They paraded her through the town finally arriving at the jailhouse. They pushed her into the cell with a shove, which caused her to fall. It was cold and musty. The smell of urine hung in the air from previous cell occupants. There were no furnishings, only a floor, walls, and cell door. Every inch of every surface was soiled and sickening. She was loath to touch any-thing or sit anywhere, yet she knew she could not stand forever. She squatted with her feet flat, her head on her knees.

Like a lotus bloom in the mud, Madeleine was a spot of pure beauty surrounded by ugliness. But it was not her bleak and gloomy circumstances that concerned her. Her mind, first and foremost, turned to Steffan. She had been denied the opportunity to say goodbye or explain to him what was happening. *God only knows what they're telling him.* She worried that they would turn him out into the street, or hand him over as an indentured serv-ant. Her heart broke. *My son, my son...* Her lips moved as she whispered silently over and over, her body rocking back and forth on her heels.

Her mind then wandered to Chelsea and the other women. Would Peggy be able to identify anyone else? Would she herself be able to keep mum when subjected to interrogation and possible torture? She felt hollow, devoid of even the strength to hold her body up. She rolled into the fetal position, unable to defend herself against the contaminated floor.

She lay there for what seemed an eternity. She had no way of telling time; there were no windows to judge whether it was day or night. She had stumbled upon a pot for relieving herself, and a jar of water. Her stomach growled off and on to let her know her normal schedule of meals had been missed.

Her mind started to go sideways, losing its grip on reality. Her dream world began to bleed into her waking life. She was having visual and audi-tory hallucinations. It was hellish in a way only people subjected to extended solitary confinement could understand. She was desperate for any stimula-tion.

When the men came to take her before the judge, she felt as much relief as fear. They summoned her forth from her cell. Her legs were already weaker from not standing and not walking. They commented on her foul-ness, ordering her to stand several feet away from them. They led her up the stairs and into the courtroom.

The days she had spent in that environment left her looking unkempt, part wild animal, part insane person. Her beauty was obscured by filth. Her appearance, which just days before had elicited admiration, now conjured feelings of disgust and revulsion. It was easy to condemn her.

The line of questioning was designed to lead her into a trap. The very structure of the questions made it impossible to answer without implicating herself or others. Desensitized to injustice and indifferent to the truth, her accusers were only concerned with putting on a public display of her crimes and fulfilling their moral duty to condemn her. They cast themselves as heroes, protecting society from evil. These pretentious guardians of morality chose their victims from the fringes of society, indicting those too poor to afford counsel, fabricating charges that were impossible to rationally defend. Madeleine was their perfect prey.

The interrogation began. She tried to answer their accusations, but the more she said, the more they twisted her words. She remained silent when they demanded to know the names of the other attendees. She tried to hold the line and protect their identities. She prayed all of this would stop, that it was just a nightmare from which she would awaken. It wasn't.

They continued to break her down with double meanings, false allegations, and entrapment. Her words began to falter. She found herself slipping and divulging information she had intended not to share. The longer it went on, the more confused she became. In spite of these slip-ups, she believed her resolve remained sturdy. But then they identified her Achilles heel.

It was brought to the counselor's attention that Madeleine had a male child. He smiled gleefully at the news, fully prepared to use him as a pawn. Armed with this information, he crafted the perfect plan to lure Madeleine into his web. He proposed a deal with the devil, a double bind in which she could only lose.

He offered her son in exchange for the name of the person who had invited her to the witches' gathering. Her heart stopped. Throughout the process, it had not occurred to her that Steffan would be used against her. She had not let herself imagine that he would be implicated for being the offspring of a witch, or that he would suffer directly for her misfortunes. They had won.

She stood silently, wrestling with her soul. There was only one choice to be made. She had always known she would gladly give her own life for that of her child, but now she was being asked to give the life of another. It was a horrifying dilemma of inconceivable proportions. And yet the choice was made before the offer had even passed from her accuser's lips.

"My son!" she wailed. "My son… I will tell you anything."

For the second time in her life, Madeleine dissociated. She watched and heard herself answering her accuser's questions, emotionless and defenseless like a sheep led to slaughter. She gave up names, places, times, and the nature of the rituals. It all spilled forth from her—yet not from her—from the Madeleine way down there in the courtroom. She remained far away, looking on as if it were happening to someone else.

When it was over, she shuffled numbly out of the court, unable to lift her head. She could not bear to look at the disappointed faces of her peers. A different kind of shame settled over her. She had betrayed all that she held dear. She was defeated.

Even at that moment, a host of heavenly beings surrounded her, pressing in to hold her and love her. They longed for her to hear them saying, "It's all an illusion. You are innocent." But she could not hear it, and she could not feel it. Waves of guilt and shame drowned out all higher awareness. She felt disconnected from all that is good and sacred. Her transgression was unforgivable. There was no hope of being reunited with Oneness.

The brief moment of enlightenment she had experienced following the goddess circle evaporated. A sinister force, silently working to keep her trapped in her current level of consciousness, had pulled her back into its dark grasp of illusion.

She was returned to the brothel, absolved of her crimes. They brought Steffan to her.

"Mama!" he cried as she rushed to hold him.

She clung to him tightly as tears streamed down her face. She loved him so much. She felt what seemed like happiness begin to surface, but she quickly remembered the sacrifice she had made. The conflict of her guilt would not permit her to feel joy. Her love for her son was now laced with something poisonous. In the hidden places of her psyche, the places so hidden that she herself could never find them, she secretly blamed her son for being the reason she had betrayed the only true friend she had ever had. Her ocean of love now contained an undercurrent of resentment.

Steffan had been well taken care of in her absence. He was friendly and sweet, popular among the other residents. Several women took turns looking after him. They did it for him, but they also did it for Madeleine.

Peggy's moment in the limelight faded almost instantaneously, and she was now seen as a snitch, not to be trusted. She was ostracized and scorned by guests and housemates alike. The only exception was the madam of the house, who gave her somewhat preferential treatment. It wasn't that she respected or liked Peggy but she tolerated her disagreeable and pandering nature in reciprocity for her blind loyalty. A mole can be useful to a person in charge.

It was agreed that everything would go back to business as usual. But of course, nothing was really the same. Madeleine was sullen now. A heavy blanket of sadness had settled over her. She went through the motions of her job, entertaining gentlemen callers, performing her chores, and taking care of Steffan, but she herself was vacant. Ever since her confession, she had not fully reentered her body.

News came of Chelsea's arrest. Madeleine heard it, but she did not respond. She walked to her room and sat on the bed, staring blankly at the wall. Steffan walked in behind her, wanting her to play a game.

"Not now, Steffan."

He made several attempts to vie for her attention. He sensed that she needed a distraction. But nothing he did got through to her. She was far, far away.

Her guilt was palpable. It exuded from every pore of her body and spread all around her like a contagion. Steffan could feel it ,but was unable to discern where it came from. As his mirror neurons came into resonance with his mother's energy, his neurology replicated her emotional state inside of himself. It felt like it was his guilt, and he wondered if his mother's sadness was somehow his fault. But Steffan's pain went completely unnoticed by his mother. She had sacrificed everything to be with him, but she could no longer enjoy him or even engage with him. She became a ghost—and he became invisible.

Madeleine wished she could have shut her ears to the news of Chelsea, but talk was everywhere. She learned that Chelsea had stood proud and unapologetic, challenging her accusers' true motives. She knew they sought to protect the interests of the church and the establishment. They exercised no empathy or integrity in their agenda of domination and control. She was calm throughout the trial. At all times, she remained connected to her higher self, rising above the corruption and treachery, tapping into and radiating the peace that passes understanding. She was not threatened by these men. She felt no need to defend against their false accusations. She stood for and spoke the truth, regardless of the consequences. They could kill her body, but they could not kill her, for she was something so much greater.

The counselor and the judge found her honesty to be an affront to their superior religious knowledge. They judged her refusal to admit guilt as pride, an unwillingness to bow her head to authority. Having assigned themselves as the spokesmen for God, they equated her actions with an unwillingness to bow before God himself, the ultimate act of rebellion and blasphemy. To presume she could bypass the church to commune with God directly was surely sufficient evidence that she was a witch. For them to place the souls of other men in danger by permitting her to roam free and spread the work of the devil would be dangerous and irresponsible on their part. She must be stopped. She must be made an example of.

She must be burned at the stake.

Out of their mercy, they would kill her slowly to give her an opportunity to see the error of her ways and repent of her sins, that even yet her soul might be saved. They exacted their revenge in the name of charity.

When they had satisfied themselves, she walked out of the courtroom with head held high. She had revealed nothing to betray her sisters. She had done nothing to compromise her integrity. She was clear that this life is an illusion and that to cling to it was like grasping at smoke or vapor. She could let it go. She could accept whatever fate might bring, because she knew that what she possessed inside—her connection to Spirit—was the only thing that was real. They could not touch the part of her that really mattered.

The date was set for Chelsea's execution. Madeleine felt sick every time she heard any mention of it. Even more disturbing was the excitement she heard in people's voices. They spoke of it like it was a show or sporting event. *What is wrong with people?* This life continued to erode her soul.

Everything inside of Madeleine dreaded going to the burning. Dreaded it—yet something also compelled her to go. She longed to tell Chelsea how sorry she was, to beg for her forgiveness. In the end, the part of her that yearned for absolution pulled her to the town square on the morning of the final judgement.

As soon as Chelsea was brought out for public display, Madeleine rushed over to her and fell down on her knees.

"I'm sorry! Please forgive me. Please forgive me. I'm so sorry. Please forgive me!"

Looking down at her with compassion, Chelsea replied, "All is forgiven, for there was never anything to forgive. I have been chosen as the voice of the One true God. I have surrendered to Divine will. Go in peace, sister."

Madeleine wished Chelsea had rained down her wrath and fury upon her. Guilt requires punishment. She felt a deep-seated need to suffer for her sins. Instead, she had been met with forgiveness and grace. Her heart shattered into a million pieces. She was grateful for this unexpected and undeserved kindness, but she could not truly receive it or let it in. In the presence of Chelsea's unwavering goodness, Madeleine felt even more unworthy.

As she lifted her head and looked at Chelsea, Madeleine's eyes were full of remorse and torment. Chelsea met her gaze with mercy and love. As they pulled Chelsea away, Madeleine remained on her knees, sobbing. After a while, she got up and walked away, unable to watch what came next. She later heard that Chelsea sang and spoke blessings as the flames consumed her. Then it was over.

Chapter 25

Return to Innocence

Sophie sat on the plane replaying all the deliciousness of her vacation. It had been perfect in every conceivable way. From lying on the beach to talking with Wendy to you-know-what with Jackson, the entire trip had been richly satisfying. She took a deep breath and let out a sigh as a smile broke across her face.

Her getaway had served to reset her whole system. She was less stressed out, less harried at work. She still gave her clients and cases her full devotion, but without needing to prove anything. By her taking things less seriously, her performance actually improved. She was friendlier, more easygoing, and simply enjoyed life more.

She didn't forget about her conversations with Wendy. She still knew there were unhealed wounds inside of her, and a wounded inner child that needed to be addressed. But she was more connected and in tune with herself now, and she intuitively knew that she would know when the time was right.

Rather than falling into a relationship with the next guy that came along, she consciously took a break from dating, choosing to make herself and her healing journey a priority. For the first time, she was truly comfortable being alone. She still felt that gnawing, empty feeling come up from time to time, but she was learning to process her emotions rather than becoming overwhelmed and suppressing them. She had a network of healers and practitioners that she could turn to for help if she felt a disturbance in the force. They were magnificent people with magnificent tools, and she was learning how to use some of them.

She immersed herself in energy, sound, and other clearing modalities until she hit a plateau. They were each helpful in their own right, but she had reached a new level, and these modalities were not able to take her where she needed to go next.

Sophie and Wendy had remained in contact after her trip. Their friendship had matured, and their conversations had more substance. In college, they had talked about boys and bars and gossip. Now they conversed about health tips, emotional intelligence, and spirituality. They were no longer satisfied to be absorbed in entertainment or academic competition. They genuinely cared about improving their lives and being the best version of themselves, mentally, emotionally, and spiritually. They could talk for hours and never ran out of things that were interesting to both of them.

Sophie told her about the diminishing return on her healing journey. Wendy explained that, while receiving passive clearings and techniques are extremely helpful, at some point, we are required to step into a more active role in our process.

"It is *your* healing journey, after all," Wendy told her.

"I was afraid you were going to say that." Sophie laughed.

"Don't shoot the messenger," Wendy said jokingly.

Wendy was just a couple of steps ahead of Sophie on the road to enlightenment. She could empathetically relate to what she was going through while still serving as an intuitive and informed guide.

"You know that I know that you know what I'm going to recommend," she continued.

"I know, I know. Hypnotherapy," Sophie said.

"Aren't you a good little listener? I've taught you so well," Wendy teased.

Sophie had already been feeling the call. She promised to do her due diligence and find a Wendy-approved practitioner. Hypnotists come in all sizes and flavors, and Wendy wanted to help Sophie find someone who would give her a deep and transformative experience.

It took her a couple of weeks to follow through on her promise. She had several deadlines at work, and there was still a part of her that was hesitant to take the plunge. Most of her wanted to embrace the process, but she could also feel a pull in the other direction—a part that would derail her plans if given the opportunity. This internal conflict waged a small battle within her. She would later learn how these self-sabotaging subconscious parts have a mind of their own and can often win the war. Eventually, Sophie's spirit prevailed, and she called to make the appointment.

* * *

The day she walked into the hypnotherapist's office, she thought she knew what to expect. Wendy had explained her sessions and Sophie thought she had a handle on it. She was soon to learn that a cognitive understanding did not translate to the emotional and visceral experience. It was one of those things she had to experience for herself. Words couldn't do that for her. Words dance around and point to the thing, but they are not the thing.

The session started off with Cheryl asking Sophie questions about what she wanted to work on or improve. Cheryl knew how to get to the heart of the matter and identified patterns in her relationships that no one had ever explained to her before. She explained the difference between the conscious and subconscious mind and that understanding the issue logically does not always mean we are able to change it where it counts, in the subconscious.

"You see, the subconscious mind isn't logical. It processes information as pictures, movies, symbolism, and emotion. So, when we try to change how we feel by using words and logic, it's like trying to explain something in English to someone who only speaks Japanese or German. You can say the same thing a hundred times, but you're never going to get anywhere. When we finally learn to communicate with the subconscious in the language it understands, change happens quickly and easily. Does that make sense?" Cheryl asked.

"I think so," Sophie answered.

Sophie was dealing with a lot of anxiety that didn't seem to be related to anything tangible that was going on in her life currently. Cheryl probed deeper, asking about Sophie's childhood, in particular her relationship with her mother. As she listened, she would interject observations and awarenesses of what may have been set up in Sophie's psyche as a result of the circumstances she'd had to deal with as a child.

She spoke to Sophie's particular situation. "When we grow up in an unstable or volatile environment, we learn to be *on guard* all the time. We never know when or where the next outburst is coming from, so we are constantly walking on eggshells and looking over our shoulder. Over time, our nervous system gets set to a baseline of anxiety. It becomes our way of being."

Sophie took all of this in. It made a lot of sense.

Cheryl continued, "The subconscious mind has infinite processing power. It keeps all of our memories constantly alive, like fully immersive 3D movies playing in the background on a loop. Until we neutralize and heal our traumas, it's like they're still happening. They continue to have the same effect as if they were happening in real time."

"Wow. That's intense," Sophie responded.

"Yeah, I know," Cheryl agreed. "You can see why it's hard to reason your way around something like that."

After hearing about Sophie's childhood and adult traumas, Cheryl took a moment to look her in the eye and said, "I'm really sorry you went through that."

Sophie could feel Cheryl's genuine empathy and care. She felt seen and understood. In just moments, Cheryl had been able to establish a sense of safety and trust that would take most people months or years to foster.

Cheryl helped Sophie gain insight into why her mother, Justine, was the way she was. Sophie told her briefly what she knew about her mom's childhood and family dynamics. Cheryl pointed out several of the coping mechanisms and patterns Justine had likely taken on as a result of being judged, rejected, and made to feel that she was never good enough. In many ways, Justine was an emotional cripple with severe abandonment issues.

For the first time, Sophie's eyes were opened to seeing her mother as damaged and reacting from hurt. It was a huge insight that helped her to put things in perspective and not take things so personally. Justine had been desperately trying to feel loved and had no idea of how to achieve that, much less love herself. Sophie realized all the conclusions she had reached about what her mother's behavior meant didn't actually mean that at all. Sophie had shifted into a new paradigm of awareness.

Cheryl proceeded to break down what she called the devil's triangle. "In dysfunctional relationships, we rotate through the various roles of being the victim, judging our abuser, and then turning around and rescuing or enabling the person who hurt us. These co-dependent cycles can go on for years. Round and round the mulberry bush, we go." She laughed to break the tension.

Sophie could see how she had cycled over and over through the roles of victim, judge ,and rescuer. For the first time, she could see why her life had been so tumultuous and chaotic. She understood why she had put up with mistreatment and clung so pathetically to her abusers. She was finally able to stop judging herself, and instead, see herself through the eyes of compassion. That alone was a huge gift.

And the session proper hadn't even started.

"Strap in and hold on," Cheryl joked as they began the hypnosis process.

Cheryl took her on a journey of healing and neutralizing the emotional impact of several key traumatic memories. This was the experiential part of the session, where changes were made in Sophie's subconscious mind. She was guided to change the verbal, emotional and visual content of a handful of pivotal negative memories. These changes were so radical that they obliterated the old synaptic pathways and neurological associations, so that she would be unable to reconstruct the trauma or its impact in the same way ever again. The old negative memories were neutralized, and in their place were positive emotions with positive visual associations.

When Sophie emerged from the hypnotherapy process, she felt as if she were born anew. She felt lighter, as if a huge weight had been lifted from her shoulders. She felt a peace and calm in her chest where the anxiety used to reside. The process itself had been quite a roller coaster ride, going into the heavy emotions she had experienced as a young girl, talking intimately with her younger self, reintegrating her inner child, and resolving the painful impressions and relationships that had shaped her fragile sense of self.

She wiped away a few tears that remained on her cheeks. It had been challenging, but it was so worth it. She had gone into the fire and come out a changed person. No longer was she trying to repress her emotions or mask her self-doubt. They were simply gone.

"Wow, that was better than sex!" Sophie laughed. "I'm still in the after-glow. It was definitely intense."

Cheryl gave her a few moments to gather herself. Then she explained that the session wasn't really over when it ended.

"You'll continue to integrate these changes over the next few days while you're sleeping. We gave your subconscious mind a lot of new information, and it will apply these changes to other memories behind the scenes. There's nothing you need to do consciously to make this happen. Your only home-work is to be kind to yourself while your subconscious mind makes these changes for you."

Sophie felt more relaxed than she could ever remember feeling. She also felt a little tired. It had been work of sorts, but the return on investment was undeniably worth it.

She scheduled a follow-up session in two weeks. That would give her time to process the changes that had been set in motion and to know what had been resolved and what still needed to be addressed.

Sophie felt like something big had happened, although she couldn't put her finger on what exactly it was. She remembered something Cheryl had said. "When we delete old programs, it's like trying to notice what's not there." She used the example of someone with chronic knee pain. "When their knee is hurting, it's all they can think about. When it stops hurting, it's the last thing they're thinking about."

That's it. The background static of anxiety that had been her constant companion was simply gone, replaced with a golden yet unfamiliar silence. She no longer had to manage her anxiety, coach herself through the next meeting, or try to talk herself down from the cliff. It was finally safe to be present. It was kind of weird, but she actually felt comfortable in her own skin.

Chapter 26

Integration

Sophie's initial high faded over time. It wasn't that the results of her initial session weren't permanent; they were. However, once she had overcome the bigger traumas, smaller ones surfaced and came to her attention. It was as if she now had the bandwidth to address issues that had previously remained on the back burner.

Now that she was no longer suppressing her emotions, she noticed certain personalities at work triggering her. She felt more annoyed than she cared to admit. The final straw was a snide comment from Brigette. She had pretended not to notice her disrespect for the last time.

"You know, Brigette, it's a shame that someone of your breeding and education wasn't taught better manners—a most unfortunate oversight on the part of your..." She paused. "...custodians." Sophie stared her in the eye unflinchingly.

Brigette was taken aback. She had grown accustomed to Sophie meekly remaining dumb whenever she had made jokes at her expense. She had mistakenly assumed that Sophie wasn't quick-witted enough to engage in verbal sparring. She could not have known that it was Sophie's unconscious fear of retribution that had caused her to keep her mouth shut. Nevertheless, by never standing up for herself, Sophie had inadvertently taught Brigette that it was okay to pick on her. But now Sophie had healed those old programs. She was no longer controlled by her own fear.

Sophie was as surprised as Brigette at her spicy response. When one's pendulum has swung too far out of balance in one direction, it often swings too far in the opposite before coming to rest in a state of balance. Sophie unleashed a beast of pent-up anger and resentment.

It felt good to speak her mind at last. She was sick to death of Brigette's passive-aggressive play for dominance. Over the next couple of weeks, she indulged in sarcastic behavior bordering on rudeness. While it was thera-peutic, in a way, to speak her truth after suppressing her voice for so long, she didn't always feel good about it afterwards. She wasn't sure she liked the person she was becoming. She didn't actually want to be unkind or hurtful like so many of the people who had hurt her in the past.

As she reflected on the good and the bad of what was emerging, she realized it might be something she wanted to address in her work with hyp-notherapy. When she shared her observations with Cheryl, she was not met with judgement of any kind.

"We all have different parts of our subconscious," Cheryl explained. "It's kind of like we all multiple personalities," she said jokingly. "Kidding, not kidding."

Sophie didn't know what she was talking about and stared at her, con-fused.

"You can think of these parts as managers in control of the various as-pects of your life. They all have a positive intention, like to help you feel safe or feel loved, but they can be pretty confused about how to go about doing their job.

"Say there's a little girl whose parents work all the time, so she feels sad and lonely. On the weekends, she goes to her grandma's house. Grandma always dotes on her and makes her feel loved and special, and…" Cheryl paused, "…Grandma always makes chocolate chip cookies. In this little girl's mind, love and cookies go together." She placed her palms together.

"Relatable," Sophie interjected.

"Now imagine she grows up and has a weight problem, but every time she feels lonely, this part of her subconscious, just wanting her to feel Grandma's love, compels her to eat cookies— cause it thinks there's love in them cookies." Cheryl animated her discourse with a funny face and accent. "Of course, cookies never loved anyone, so it's never going to work, but this part of her mind, with its one little tool in its toolbox, will keep trying 'til the cows come home."

Cheryl looked to see if Sophie was registering what she was saying. "Remember, the subconscious mind isn't logical. But it does kind of make sense once you understand how it works."

Sophie nodded. "I can see that."

"I know you're feeling bad about the situation at the office but I want you to understand that the part of you that keeps firing off at Brigette isn't bad, per se. It does have a positive intention—although, let's face it, it may be a little misguided." Cheryl's tone and body language reassured her, while simultaneously acknowledging that her behavior wasn't necessarily cool.

Over several sessions, layers of the onion were peeled away. Sophie began to integrate the fractured, disowned, and conflicting parts of herself. She was becoming more whole within as she integrated all of the little Sophies inside of her with compassion and understanding.

What happened next came as a surprise. While Cheryl had worked with past life regression in her hypnosis work, she focused primarily on assisting her clients to resolve current life trauma. Occasionally, however, the subconscious mind takes charge and guides the client where it knows they need to go for resolution. It can take the client off script, so to speak, to an unforeseen destination.

Cheryl was an excellent detective. She saw the subconscious as a puzzle or a riddle to be solved. The more she had worked with clients, common patterns had emerged that had now become easy for her to identify. Having an astute understanding of the subconscious mind, its patterns and programs, she was usually able to identify the source of her clients' issues through conversation and in-depth inquiry. However, on occasion, the root cause eluded her. This was one of those times.

Many layers of Sophie's emotional turmoil had been lifted and cleared. But she had an untoward level of guilt, which had been tenacious and unrelenting. Together, they had addressed the guilt she had felt as a child and even as an infant, rising from unprovoked anger and rejection from her mother. They had also looked at the misplaced guilt she had felt as a result of her relationships with Alex and Simon. However, a piece of the puzzle was still missing. Cheryl knew from experience that, in these situations, she must call on the subconscious to share its secrets and show them what they didn't know that they didn't know.

Cheryl guided her into hypnosis and had her think about the feeling of guilt and the situations in her life that triggered it. Getting in touch with the feeling in a powerful way was to serve as a homing beacon back to the first time she had ever felt this guilt. Letting go of all preconceived notions of where her subconscious mind would take her, she was to simply follow its lead and allow it to guide her back to a memory that was relevant to this emotion of guilt.

She traveled through the tunnels of time and popped into a scene in which nothing was familiar. She was hunched over on the ground, sobbing. There were voices all around her, jeering and yelling threats. As she looked down, she could see that she was wearing a full-length dress, its hem covered in dirt. Her hands were shaking. She felt overwrought with grief and sadness.

Cheryl gently probed into the scene, asking her questions about what she saw, who was there and what she was feeling.

"Is this a memory from this life, or is it a former incarnation?" Cheryl asked.

As soon as she heard the question, Sophie was no longer disoriented. She realized she had regressed into a past life. She looked up and saw the face of the most peaceful, loving human being. She had never seen this woman before, but she knew that she knew her. The woman looked at her with the purity and grace of an angel. *"All is forgiven,"* she heard her say. Sophie felt a deep pain in her chest as tears rolled down her face.

"I'm around a lot of people. They're angry and yelling. There's a woman above me. She looks very kind, and she is saying all is forgiven. I did something to her. I hurt her," Sophie relayed to Cheryl.

It all came crashing into her awareness with crystal-clear understanding.

"I betrayed her. She's going to be put to death because of something I said. I caused this. It's all my fault."

Sophie was fully associated into this scene, feeling the depth of emotion this former self was feeling in every minute detail. She was overwhelmed and began to break down. Cheryl told her to open her eyes to dissociate and gather herself. She guided her, with Emotional Freedom Techniques, to release enough of the emotion to continue on. Closing her eyes once again, Sophie returned to the scene, still in hypnosis.

Cheryl could see at once that this past life was the root cause of Sophie's guilt. She had Sophie visualize her current life self entering this situation and comforting her former incarnation. Sophie held space to allow this woman, this other aspect of herself, to verbalize everything she was feeling, so that she finally felt understood. Cheryl walked Sophie through the process of hugging this variation of her inner child and giving her the resources she needed to see things from a higher perspective. By the end of the process, the young woman was able to truly integrate self-forgiveness and let go of her crushing guilt.

When Sophie came out of hypnosis, she and Cheryl discussed some of the lessons and insights Sophie had gained from the session. Sophie had heard of reincarnation, but had never given it much thought. Before that day, she wasn't even sure if she believed in it. However, the intensity and realness of this experience were compelling. It would have been nearly impossible to persuade her that it was merely her imagination. She was—or had been—this other woman, and she was certain that she had given both of them a tremendous gift of healing that day.

Her perspective on life shifted spontaneously as a result of her experience. She saw it as kind of like a dream or a movie. *It feels real, but it's not real.* Somehow, she understood that it was the soul lessons and wisdom that mattered. They were eternal. The tragedies were not.

The session had been a total success. Her misplaced false guilt had vanished. But what did it really mean that she had lived another lifetime, and how in the world could this person, in another time and place, have such a profound impact on her current life? And if she could travel, so to speak, back in time to help this other self, then what was time?

Sophie's past life regression opened up an existential rabbit hole. Questions about the nature of reality, where souls came from, why they were here, and what it all meant flooded her consciousness. It was mind-bending, bizarre, and frankly a little too much.

Chapter 27

Down the Rabbit Hole

After just a few sessions with Cheryl, Sophie's internal thermostat had been completely reset. Her emotional baseline was calm and relaxed. Her unworthiness, which had been primarily a result of her guilt, had all but vanished, and her abandonment issues were practically nonexistent. She now knew who she was, and she liked who she was.

All of her relationships became more pleasant. She was even beginning to get along with Brigette. She didn't have to forcefully set boundaries. The change was organic. Her energy had noticeably shifted, and people just naturally treated her better. She also noticed that new people who came into her life were of a higher caliber. They were more conscious and self-aware. They expressed empathy and compassion for others. It was as if she had shifted into a parallel reality.

All of this freed up more bandwidth for her to go deeper into spirituality and her relationship with Source. She began to research several religions, including Buddhism, Hinduism, and Gnosticism. There were similarities throughout, and of course, differences as well. Often, it seemed they were saying the same thing with different words. Christianity confused her the most. The idea that God had created man, yet could condemn him to suffer in hell for eternity for a small infraction seemed unjust and cruel. She remembered her pastor from childhood saying that "God's ways are higher than our ways." But frankly, that felt like doublespeak, an elaborate justification for some psychopathic entity posing as God.

As she continued her search, it felt like some of her questions were answered, while other answers remained elusive. She resonated with the Buddhist concepts of non-attachment and non-resistance.. But she also resonated with the Hindu concepts that God is in all, as all, and that humans are intrinsically divine as an expression of the one divinity. And after her past life regression, she was definitely on board with their belief in reincarnation. She was particularly intrigued by their teachings about samsara, the wheel of reincarnation, in which souls continuously reincarnate based on their karma until they achieve enlightenment.

She was trying to put it all together to form a mental map of how it worked, how humans got here, and what it actually meant to achieve liberation. It was a complex puzzle, and there were a lot of moving parts. One question prevailed: *Why is it so hard?* If enlightenment was the goal, then why was it so elusive, its achievement shrouded in mystery and secrecy? Humans had definitely not been given a clear roadmap to follow. How could someone know if they were on the right path? Did all paths lead to the same destination? How did someone go about clearing their karma? It felt as if the entire human race was caught in a maze of confusion, with endless false trails, and in the end, no exit. It felt like a big cosmic joke.

While she was in alignment with the Hindu teaching that we are, in our essence, divine, it was difficult to reconcile with the darkness that seemed to be so pervasive in human nature. Most humans did not appear or act divine, by a long shot. They were petty and selfish at best, cruel and manipulative at worst. Some even ventured into the waters of pure evil. How could divine beings have become so corrupt? These weren't just philosophical questions; they weighed heavily on her heart.

But at least now, she was strong enough internally and had the emotional fortitude to entertain these questions. Previously, she had been trapped in survival mode, all of her energy spent on coping with dysfunctional relationships and trying to suppress her unresolved traumas. If she had pondered these painful dilemmas of the human condition before, it would have sent her into a state of utter despair. But she was now healed enough to take these questions on without becoming overwhelmed, and to approach them from a somewhat objective place.

Sophie's world was shifting around her. She had moments where she felt in tune with something greater than herself, connected to a goodness that began to make itself known. She observed many synchronicities she hadn't noticed before. She wasn't sure if they had always been happening, and she had just been oblivious, or if some force was truly beginning to conspire on her behalf. She started to feel safer, like she was being taken care of somehow, and began to ease into a trust that things were working out for her good. In her personal experience, at least, the universe was transforming from a hostile environment into a supportive one.

Through a series of coincidences, Sophie was introduced to a meditation practice. A woman she had met in yoga class told her about it. The more she talked, the more Sophie lit up inside. It felt like this was the answer to her unspoken prayers. It held the answers to her questions about the problem of the human condition and the promise of how to evolve beyond it.

Over the next few weeks, Sophie learned many spiritual principles that gave her a lot of clarity. She was learning to meditate in a practice that gave her access to her higher self in a tangible way. She could feel when she was connected, and she was learning how to channel information from the higher dimensions. Having access to higher wisdom and guidance was the missing piece that she had needed for clear direction.

The instructor, Colleen, explained that we are multidimensional beings with many levels of awareness. Some aspects of ourselves, even though they are higher than our conscious awareness, are still subject to the distortion of the collective unconscious. Other aspects of ourselves are of such a high vibration that they are above corruption, confusion, and half-truths. The line of demarcation, so to speak, is at the level of Christ consciousness. Anything not of Christ consciousness is subject to distortion; anything of Christ consciousness is pure truth and perfection.

In meditation, Sophie learned how to connect with this pure and perfect aspect of herself. Channeling from this level, she could trust that the messages and guidance she received were reliable, safe, and of the highest truth. She learned how to safeguard against her own ego's distortion as the message was filtered down through the layers of her consciousness. Having a direct personal connection served to at least eliminate the distortions that could be added by the egos of others. She hadn't been wrong in thinking this reality is complex and full of pitfalls, and it was a huge relief to learn tools to protect herself, and others, from these perils.

Chapter 28

Still Just a Girl

As much as these topics and questions dominated her thought life, Sophie was still just a girl living a normal life. She wanted the same things most girls want: a boyfriend, fun, passion, intimacy. She found her thoughts wandering back to Robert. He had been one of the few bright spots in her life, a splash of color on a blank canvas, showing her what joy felt like. He had shown her that it was possible to be swept off your feet and grounded simultaneously. He had been balanced and stable, yet free. Now she was becoming that person. She was as light as she was solid.

She wasn't seriously pursuing romance, though she did go on a few dates here and there. Her old self would have probably fallen into a relationship with any number of these eligible bachelors, but now she was able to discern, within just a few minutes, if their vibration was a match for her own. She couldn't put into words exactly what it was she was looking for, nor could she describe what it was about these men that wasn't a fit. But she did know what it felt like to be in the presence of a like-minded soul.

She met him in a yoga class. He was filling in as a substitute instructor. For Sophie, yoga class was a come-as-you-are affair. She showed up with no makeup, raw and ready to sweat. She was not prepared to be confronted with an uber-hot guy.

She side-glanced at a couple of the other women. "Oh my god," she mouthed silently as she widened her eyes and tilted her head in his direction. She was quick to look down as soon as he turned around, but she was pretty sure she had been busted.

Sophie's weight had stabilized on her journey of self-love and acceptance. She was no longer living, eating, or not eating to please other people or to meet their expectations. Her lifestyle and diet were now a way to connect with herself. It was a part of being authentic and congruent with her new self-concept as a divine feminine being. That said, she still had an intact ego that wanted to look attractive and get noticed. She was a vivacious, hot-blooded woman who had sexual needs and passions. This man was definitely a head-turner and she felt a ripple of desire well up inside of her.

As soon as class started, she was engaged in her yoga practice. The rigor of the sessions demanded that she be fully present. It was its own form of meditation.

When the class was over, several of the other women went up to thank the instructor, AKA Hot Teacher. She overheard them inquiring where he taught on a regular basis. She wanted to go talk to him as well, but found she was feeling a bit shy. *That's interesting.* She hadn't felt this way around a man since the early days of college.

She was one of the last to pack up and leave.

He walked over to introduce himself. Hi, my name is Mark."

"Pleasure to meet you," she responded. "I'm Sophie."

"Do you make these classes often?" he inquired.

"About three days a week."

"Awesome. Mandy asked me to fill in for her a couple times a week. She has some family stuff going on. Hopefully, I'll see you again," Mark added. He held her gaze, giving her a warm smile.

"I look forward to it," Sophie responded, smiling shyly. She could feel herself blushing.

Why is it so hard to look straight at him and why am I blushing? She felt slightly annoyed with herself. *He's just being polite, Sophie. Be cool.*

He wasn't just being polite. She had caught his eye, and he was feeling the same way. He exuded a quiet confidence, a magnetic masculinity without the toxicity she had encountered so many times before. In spite of her butterflies, she also felt a centered calmness in him. He was one of those rare individuals with an organically good energy. In the yoga and spiritual community, Sophie had come across some people who had a forced or fake positivity. It always felt incongruent and disjointed, as if they knew what spirituality was supposed to look like, but they hadn't done the deeper work to integrate it authentically. Mark was not one of those people. His energy was clear and smooth. He didn't have to put on confidence like a dinner jacket. It was a part of his essence as someone who knew who he was and had made peace with his shortcomings as well as his strengths. There was something about him that Sophie wanted more of. He was someone worth getting to know.

As they shook hands, they held on a little longer than would be considered customary. They both became aware of their reluctance to let go at the same time and laughed.

"See you soon," Mark said, following her out the door with his eyes.

Sophie gave a quick glance back and a smile as she turned the corner. There was a spring in her step as she made her way to the car. *Who are you, and where have you been all my life? … I'm in trouble.*

Sophie couldn't wipe the grin off her face as she drove home. What a happy surprise the Universe had introduced to her that day. She spent a little extra time with self-care that evening. She indulged in a bubble bath. She painted her toenails. She poured herself a glass of wine and sat on her back patio, taking in the beauty of life. All was well with her world.

She made it a point to make it to yoga as many evenings as she could. It wasn't until the following Tuesday that Mark reappeared as the instructor. He gave her a lingering hug as soon as he saw her.

"It's so good to see you." He looked genuinely excited.

Sophie felt tingles go through her body as he embraced her. She had never had a reaction quite like this with anyone before. It was electric.

Most of the women in class were either married or in a relationship. Their admiration of Mark was more the way you admired a beautiful painting or piece of art. None of them would be competing for his attention.

Sophie had grown close to many of the women in her yoga class. They all thought her crush on Mark was adorable. They cheered her on, and of course, teased her about it.

"You are so hot for teacher, girl," Amanda stated, matter of factly.

"Guilty as charged," Sophie admitted, unrolling her yoga mat.

"So, when are you gonna make your move?" Amanda quizzed.

"I'm just gonna be the honey and see if the bees come to me," Sophie said with a playful grin.

"Chicken," Amanda whispered as she walked to her own mat.

After class that day, as Sophie was putting her yoga mat away, Mark struck up a conversation. They exchanged pleasantries and learned a few basic facts about each other. He had moved to the city about six months prior. Before that, he had been traveling through Thailand and India.

"They should have picked you to do that beer commercial." She laughed. "You, sir, are the most interesting man in the world." She was joking, but she meant it. The more she learned, the more wonderful he seemed. *He's an absolute dreamboat.* She felt the giddiness beginning to surface again.

"Not really. I'm actually just really lucky," he said modestly.

He didn't let her get away without making sure he had her phone number this time. He had forced himself to wait until their second meeting so as not to seem too forward or presumptuous.

"Could I talk you into joining me for dinner or a coffee sometime?" he asked.

"Yes!" she practically shouted. Realizing she sounded a bit over the moon, she lowered her voice, and with a bit more control, reiterated, "Yes, I'd love that."

Their first date was at a juice bar, a casual setting without the pressures of a fancy dinner. It was perfect. Sophie was interested in getting to know him, not in being wined and dined. The conversation flowed freely. She learned that he had grown up in California, graduated from medical school, and had his own practice for two years before becoming disenchanted with the medical establishment. From the beginning, he had noticed inconsistencies and blind spots in patient care. Increasingly, he became unable to turn a blind eye to how broken the system was. Of course, there was some good to be found in Western medicine, but by and large, the medical establishment was missing the boat. He saw patients being prescribed drugs rather than being counseled on their diet. He saw symptoms treated rather than underlying causes. He saw doctors prescribing opiates and benzodiazepines like they were candy.

When his conscience would no longer allow him to participate, he had walked away and embarked on a walkabout to find the meaning of life. He felt he needed to cleanse himself of his guilt by association. He felt dirty and used. He hadn't tried to explain it to any of his peers. They had clearly drunk the Kool-Aid. Besides, they were too financially invested to consider challenging the status quo.

Before he quit, Mark had tried to coach his clients to alter their eating and exercise habits. He had encouraged them to look at natural or alternative methods to address their anxiety and pain. But like the practitioners, they had been conditioned to take a prescription for everything. It almost felt like they had taken on a learned helplessness. Rather than take responsibility for their own care and well-being, they left it up to their doctor to fix their problems with a magic pill. He was disappointed in his patients and disillusioned by a system that had trained them to be this way. Disappointment gave way to judgement and irritation laced with disgust. Everyone seemed so brainwashed and lazy. He knew he wasn't helping anyone with his negative attitude.

He virtually ran away. It was easy enough to sell his beachfront condo. Whatever he couldn't sell, he put in storage. With what he could fit in a backpack, he boarded a plane and headed for India.

He had spent six months in an ashram, engaging in a daily practice of meditation, yoga, breath work, and free time for self-reflection. There were days when he questioned why he was there and what had possessed him to give up everything he had worked so hard for to come halfway around the world and sit cross-legged on the floor for hours. But as he persisted in going within, his mind began to clear. His heart was opening, and his energy was beginning to flow more freely. The lines of separation between himself and his world grew thinner. The more time he spent in meditation and alone in nature, the more he could feel himself merging with the Oneness. He knew that wherever he went in this world, he was at home and that he belonged.

After his time in India, he continued his journey, traveling through Thailand and Vietnam. He was fully present and enjoyed the variety of scenery, foods, cultures, and people. It was so fascinating to see the different ways people lived their lives and what life meant to them. He had been raised to view life through the lens of money, status, and success. He was learning that so much of the rest of the world placed more value on community and connection with the earth. It made him question everything he had thought was important or even real. His consciousness did a total reset. His mind was a blank slate, and he could rebuild his reality from the ground up. He could choose his self-concept and values consciously instead of inheriting the values he had been taught since childhood.

"So, what do you want to build for your life?" Sophie asked.

"To be honest, I haven't figured it all out," he replied. "I guess I'm learning to be okay with being in the question."

"I like that," Sophie said. "I could use a little more of that myself."

Sophie had never met anyone like Mark. He had figured out that life was more about being than doing, and he actually lived his life that way. It felt expansive and calming just to be in his presence. He was really and truly alive, open to possibility, free of preconceived ideas and agendas. She could feel something inside of her opening up to let in this new energy, as if something was being recoded in her awareness. It was deeper than words, but she could feel it in her mind, dissolving old patterns of thinking and creating an open space of emptiness. It felt a little weird, but she allowed herself to sit with it.

They talked for hours. So much of their communication was happening on an energetic and psychic level beyond words. They connected heart, mind, and soul. It seemed they would never run out of things to say. Sophie could have sat there forever. She felt like she had known him for eternity, and yet it all seemed so new and fresh at the same time. This was the single most amazing, wonderful, confusing, mind-blowing, profound, and satisfying encounter fate had ever brought her way. It was with reluctance that they pulled themselves away when the shop was closing.

From that day on, they became almost inseparable—not in a co-dependent way, as so many of Sophie's past relationships had been, but rather in a balanced interdependent way. They each continued to live their own lives, pursue their goals, and hang out with their friends. But the best part of their day was spending time together. There was no one and nothing they enjoyed more than being with each other—cooking, laughing, discussing ideas. As for the sex, it was almost ethereal.

Sophie had had good sex before. Hell, she had had *great* sex before. But sex with Mark was in a category all its own. It wasn't just about the physical satisfaction. There was an energy exchange that began with the first kiss and intensified throughout the arousal of foreplay and intimacy. Climax with Mark was nothing short of a spiritual experience.

Sophie had never imagined life could be this lovely. *I'm either really lucky or supremely blessed.* Later, looking back, she would realize it was largely a result of the healing she had initiated in her work with Cheryl. She wasn't just lucky; she had changed her subconscious patterns, and she was attracting better relationships all the way around. She was also able to hold a frequency that brought out the best in people who were in her energy field, rather than unconsciously triggering their wounds and traumas. She had changed, and her whole world changed around her.

Chapter 29

Falling In Love

Sophie and Mark crossed several relationship milestones. They took their first road trip together to the redwoods. It was a magical weekend. To be surrounded by trees that had been there for centuries was breathtaking.

"It kind of makes all of our ambitions and achievements seem pretty insignificant, doesn't it?" Mark commented.

Sophie, continuing to look up at the treetops, did not reply. *Wow.* She stood, and she listened. These old and giant redwoods had a message for her. They spoke of the infinite and eternal wisdom of creation and the futility of man's strivings. They spoke of the contrast between the Great Spirit that was one with all things versus man's ego that was caught up in separation and conflict. They spoke of beauty and peace and stillness. They spoke of what was real and true. All this they said without words. All this they said just by being.

She was lost in reverie for what must have been an hour or more. Mark could sense that she was processing something, so he gave her the space to do so. When he could see that she was ready to move on, he walked over to her and gently kissed her. He put his arms around her and held her close.

All he said was, "I know."

She was so grateful to be sharing this part of her life journey with him. Sharing moments like this created a richer and deeper bond. She couldn't imagine her life without him. They walked in silence, holding hands, pointing at a bird here, an interesting plant there. She was learning that he was one of those people you didn't"t have to talk to constantly. She was learning how to just be.

Another milestone was meeting each other's parents. Sophie was happy and excited to meet Mark's mother and father. They had been high school sweethearts, married for forty years now. Mark had enjoyed the proverbial apple-pie-and-white-picket-fence childhood. His parents got along, were well off, and had supported their children both financially and emotionally. They had done it right. It made sense that Mark was such a remarkable human being with so few—if any—emotional issues. *He's a freak of nature.* She smiled to herself.

Sophie had never actually seen a healthy, functional family before. It was reassuring to know that there were still a few good people left in this world. It was easy for Mark to show off his folks, knowing they would welcome Sophie with open arms. They made her feel at home right away and treated her as if she was one of the family. They trusted Mark. They had raised him, after all. If Sophie had won his heart, then she had won theirs too.

When it was her turn to introduce Mark to her parents, she had a lot of reservations. For the most part, she had come to terms with her mother's issues and had forgiven her. She had made peace with her past, but she was still nervous for Mark to see the uncensored version of her childhood. She had grown up on the other side of the tracks. Traces of embarrassment and shame still lingered.

The day they went to see her, Justine had intended to put her best foot forward. She hadn't seen her daughter in a couple of years, and she was excited and happy to spend time with her. She wanted to make Sophie proud of her and to impress her new beau. But as the hour approached, her insecurities got the best of her. She started drinking, both to quell her anxiety and to bolster her tenuous self-esteem. Inwardly, alcohol gave her a false sense of confidence and charm. But outwardly, it brought out the worst in her; her behavior became unpredictable and often ill-mannered.

By the time Sophie and Mark arrived at the door, she was halfway through a fifth of scotch. She opened the door, stumbling, slurring her words, hugging and kissing them both sloppily. Initially enthusiastic and happy, her mood turned dark when she felt Sophie bristle at her embrace.

She started her all-too-familiar victim routine. "What? You aren't happy to see your mother?"

"Not now, Mom. We just want to spend some time with you."

"Is this the handsome doctor?" She flirted shamelessly with Mark, oblivious to the inappropriateness of her behavior.

"Mom, please," Sophie pleaded.

"Don't be jealous, Butterball," Justine goaded. She had bastardized the nickname Sophie's grandmother had given her from the first moment she had learned of it.

"Really, mom?" Sophie was starting to get irritated.

"Yep, she was always jealous of her mom—weren't you, Chunky Monkey?" she sneered. She held her hand up as if to whisper to Mark. "She was always the chubby girl." Removing her hand, she added, "Better watch out you don't gain it all back."

"That's enough! How much have you had to drink?" Sophie interrupted, her voice raised. She felt her face getting hot with embarrassment and rage.

Justine did not take well to having her drinking brought into question. "Don't you come up in my house telling me how to live my life! You think you're so much better than me. Well, you're not. You think you're so high-falutin with your fancy job and your fancy boyfriend. I know who you really are."

The situation escalated from there. Once Justine had started down the path of self-pity and anger, it ran like a self-perpetuating program. Her nasty alter ego stepped in and took over the helm. No one, including herself, was able to stop it until she passed out and woke up sober once again.

"What can I help with?" Mark tried to intervene and change the subject, hoping this would set the ship aright.

"You can get me a drink." Justine gestured towards the refrigerator.

"Oh my god." Sophie rolled her eyes.

This elicited a stream of profanity and accusations that was shocking, even by Justine's standards. That was the last straw. Sophie gathered her purse and sweater and looked at Mark.

"It's no use. Let's just go."

Justine continued to hurl insults and yell at the top of her lungs as she followed them out the door and all the way down the driveway.

On the drive home, Sophie sat in stunned silence. She was utterly humiliated. She had hoped beyond hope that her mother would have been able to hold it together just this once.

"Wow… I'm sorry," Sophie said after about twenty minutes.

"Why are you sorry? You didn't do anything," Mark reassured her.

"I should have known better," she said, shrugging her shoulders.

"How could you have known?"

"Because I know my mom. Trust me, I should have known better. My childhood wasn't rainbows and ponies like yours," she said dejectedly.

Mark pulled over and stopped the car. He took Sophie's face in his hands and looked into her eyes. "I love you. Deeply. You are not your mom. You are a beautiful, strong, amazing woman, and I'm so proud of you," he said tenderly.

Sophie began to cry. She took in his love. She allowed herself to accept the truth of his words. Another layer of self-rejection and unworthiness was healed that day. He was right. She was not her mother. She was her own person. Her worthiness was not dependent on where she had come from, but on who she was now, in this moment, and where she was going. She let it all go, and she let him hold her.

Sophie trusted this man. Her darkest secrets had been exposed, and he loved her unconditionally. She had already been transparent about her past relationships. She wasn't proud of her choices, but she wasn't apologetic either. She understood the forces that had driven her past behavior, and she had done the work of facing it and healing it. She was learning to accept the truth of her innocence.

When Mark asked Sophie to move in with him, it felt like the most natural thing in the world. He already felt like her home. There was nowhere else she'd rather be.

On moving day, the dream couple crossed another milestone: their first fight. As close as their life was to heaven on Earth, they were still living in an imperfect world. Egos can get in the way of our best intentions. It started as something silly, like most fights do.

When Mark showed up to Sophie's condo with the moving truck, he was more than a little surprised at the number of boxes and stacks of clothes she had waiting to go.

"You want to take all of this?" he asked disparagingly.

"I don't want to take it, I am taking it," she replied firmly, not appreciating his tone.

"We can't possibly fit all of this in our new place," he countered.

"We'll just have to figure it out," she responded flippantly.

Mark laughed. "You need to figure out what stays and what goes."

In his travels to India and Asia, Mark had undergone a shedding of his worldly possessions and embraced a simpler lifestyle. He saw materialism as a distraction, an obstacle to letting go of attachment. Of course, he wasn't perfectly consistent in his convictions. He still had the top-of-the-line electronics and computer gadgets, things he rationalized as needing for his job. Mentally, he put those things in a different category from all the unnecessary and ridiculous stuff acquired by the public at large.

Sophie was not on board with his minimalist lifestyle. She hadn't sat for months in an ashram with no creature comforts or backpacked across Asia with just the clothes on her back. That was great for him, but it wasn't for her. She didn't appreciate Mark trying to guilt trip her into getting rid of her things. They were hers, and she needed them.

He started quizzing her as to the contents of each box, calling into question how often she used it, what it was for, and whether or not she really needed it. She had never seen him act like this. *Jesus, we haven't even moved in together yet and he's already turning into a jerk.* Flustered and annoyed, Sophie walked away. *This was a bad idea.*

She locked herself in the bathroom. She didn't trust herself not to say something mean. *Oh my god. It's happening again. I should have known it was too good to be true.* Her old pattern of waiting for the other shoe to drop kicked in, in full force. She didn't feel safe. All it had taken was this tiny misstep on Mark's part to trigger the trauma of all of her past betrayals. Tears streamed down her face.

Mark gave himself a minute to calm down before following her to the bathroom. He knocked quietly on the door.

"You okay in there?" he asked.

Sophie didn't respond. She was too fraught with emotion to say anything rational. She knew her reaction was disproportionate to the occasion but she couldn't help how she felt. It would take her a minute to sort it out. She didn't know what to say.

"Sophie, what's going on?" he prompted.

"I'm just going to the bathroom," she bluffed.

He didn't buy it. He knew she was upset. Oddly, he didn't feel bad for what he had done. He convinced himself that she was just overreacting. He didn't yet realize that from her point of view, the issue wasn't about the stuff, it was about respect and consideration. He had become locked in his masculine brain for a moment and couldn't see around his pragmatic, problem-solving approach. He found himself getting annoyed that she was stalling their progress in the moving process. *She's being ridiculous.*

They were at an impasse. He didn't want to waste any more time cajoling Sophie's whims, so he angrily began loading up the boxes. When he was done, he walked back to the bathroom door and announced loudly, "The truck is loaded. Let's go."

She came out of the bathroom trying not to look as if she had been crying. Mark took her cue and pretended not to notice. Their silence continued throughout the drive and the unloading process. They were both keenly aware that their disagreement needed to be resolved, but circumstances didn't lend themselves to a long, drawn-out, heart-to-heart discussion.

When the move was complete and the truck returned, they finally sat down to talk about what had happened. They both had enough self-awareness, emotional intelligence, and communication skills to sort out where things had gone off the rails. They were each willing to attempt, at least, to see the situation from the other person's perspective. They both took ownership of their part in it and apologized sincerely.

They had successfully navigated their first spat. It was kind of a relief to have it out of the way. It can be scary to wonder how one's partner, and indeed, one's self will handle conflict in an intimate relationship. They had handled it really well, all things considered. They had taken the opportunity to understand each other on an even deeper level.

"I like you, Mr. Giles." Sophie smiled.

"Not half as much as I like you," he replied, kissing the back of her hand.

They fell asleep in each other's arms, smiles on their faces, surrounded by tons and tons of Sophie's stuff.

Chapter 30

Two Become One

Sophie and Mark lived together for two years before he popped the question. They had gotten to know each other in every possible way. They had seen each other at their worst and best. Neither of them had any reservations about spending the rest of their lives together.

Sophie wasn't attached to the idea of marriage. She felt so deeply secure in their relationship that she didn't need a piece of paper to validate their commitment. It was more of a formality—and of course, very romantic. He wanted to show his love and devotion for her publicly. He wanted everyone in their circle to know how much he loved and honored this woman.

They set a date for late spring. She didn't stress over having every little thing a certain way. What mattered most to both of them was that they worked together to make it an intimate and enjoyable experience for each other and their friends.

When Sophie broke the news to Wendy, her best friend squealed with excitement. "Do you think you and Jeff can make it?" Sophie asked.

"Hmm, let me check. I do have an availability… I'll pencil you in," Wendy said wryly.

"Brat!" Sophie retorted.

Wendy giggled, pleased with herself. "A thousand horses couldn't keep me away," she assured her.

"Well, in that case, will you be my maid of honor?" Sophie requested.

"Of course! I'd be honored. No pun intended." She laughed.

Their friendship had remained as close as ever. They spoke at least once a week. Wendy had given up law to become a full-time hypnotherapist. Jeff was her true blue and supported her in whatever she needed to make her happy. Most of her friends and family had tried to talk her out of it. She knew that financially, it looked like a ridiculous and irresponsible decision. Sophie was the one friend who got it. Mark had essentially done the same thing, walking away from his medical practice. The soul's calling doesn't always conform to conventional wisdom.

Most of their conversations revolved around their philosophical and spiritual musings. Wendy was the trailblazer, and Sophie was one of the few people in her life who was able to keep up. Not long after Sophie had visited her that summer, Wendy had had her first astral travel experience since childhood. One morning, lying on her chaise lounge in a quiet state of reverie, she spontaneously popped out of her body. She could see herself lying on the chaise with her eyes closed. The first time was such a surprise that she immediately returned and woke up. When she realized what had happened, she couldn't wait to tell someone. Naturally, that someone had been Sophie.

So many mysteries remained. Delving into the secrets of the subconscious mind soon gives way to the Superconscious, or higher self, as some would call it. It seemed it was true that the more one learned, the more questions opened up. Sophie was starting to put the pieces together for herself of how this reality was structured, how and why souls came to be here, and what their purpose was. She had wanted to focus only on the positive aspects of spiritual awakening, but kept running into situations where it was impossible to deny "the dark side of the Force," as one might call it. Pretending it wasn't real wasn't a viable solution. Denial is not enlightenment.

Wendy flew in a couple of days early to help her with the last-minute details. Sophie wanted to relish some girl bonding time before officially getting hitched. They stayed up late, sharing stories of a more personal nature, giggling and carrying on. They swapped secrets about the men in their lives. Nothing was censored, and they never ran out of things to talk about.

"Damn, it's good to see you," Sophie said warmly.

"It's really good to see you, too," Wendy agreed. "You're getting married!" She squealed, making a silly, excited face.

"That I am." Sophie nodded. "That, I am."

* * *

The wedding went off without a hitch. The weather was perfect. The ceremony was held under a gazebo in a beautiful garden, flowers in full bloom. Sophie's dress was stunning. The gods most certainly smiled upon them that day.

They had written their own wedding vows. It was hard to put into words everything she felt about Mark. He was the most exceptional human being she had ever met—kind, intelligent, funny, handsome.

Mark had struggled equally to express the full extent of his love for his bride. After all the time they had spent together, she still took his breath away. She was an exquisite beauty, insightful, smart, and compassionate.

With steady voices, they each read their words of devotion. There was barely a dry eye in the garden that day. Everyone was swept up in their passion. It was too beautiful to bear.

The reception was fun and casual, exactly the way they had wanted it to be. Sophie's dad had done the honors of giving her away. Her relationship with her father had never been particularly close. When Sophie was growing up, her mother had made it difficult for him to spend time with her. The pain of the situation made his relationship with Sophie bittersweet. At some point, he had given up the fight, and there was a failure to bond.

Sophie had wrestled with whether to invite her mother. In the end, she had decided that it was her day, and it wasn't worth the risk of it being ruined by one of Justine's intoxicated rants. Sadly, the last trip had proven that she could still be unreliable and nasty. It wasn't that Sophie held a grudge, but on this day, she chose to honor herself by setting boundaries. Most of their close friends knew the situation. No one brought up her mother's obvious absence.

Mark's parents were pleased as punch at his choice in a bride. As accepting and supportive as they were, even they had been challenged by his surprising decision to walk away from his career as a physician. They had been relieved when he had returned to his roots and once again chosen to practice medicine in a way that aligned with his values.

Everyone ate, drank, and danced the night away. There were toasts and hugs and laughter. Mark's parents shared their wedding present during their toast: a surprise honeymoon in Bali. They were to fly out the next day. Everyone cheered. Sophie hugged her new in-laws.

"Thank you! You shouldn't have but I'm really glad you did," Sophie said, laughing.

After all the festivities were over and the last guest had gone, Mark and Sophie crawled into bed exhausted. As wonderful as it had been, they were both relieved it was over. Their heads barely hit the pillow before they were drifting off to sleep.

"Goodnight, Mr. Giles," Sophie whispered.

"Goodnight, Mrs. Giles," Mark replied with a grin.

Sophie smiled to herself. *Mrs. Giles.* She liked the sound of that.

The next thing she knew, the alarm was ringing.

Chapter 31

Deeper Down The Rabbit Hole

They returned from Bali and settled into everyday life. Having integrated holistic health into his medical practice, Mark was very engaged in his work. He felt connected to his patients and was personally invested in their well-being. He was always searching for answers and looking at cutting-edge research to expand his knowledge. In this pursuit, he frequently attended conferences and lectures.

It was at one such conference that his mind was stretched beyond anything he could have imagined. The speaker presented studies that indicated that memory and cellular health were held outside the body in a quantum field of information that neurons and DNA tuned into for instruction. This was a mind-blowing perspective that turned his current understanding upside down.

In his personal life, he had studied the laws of attraction and manifestation. He had a simplistic understanding of the quantum field of potential and how humans could draw forth their desired reality through visualization and affirmations. He had had some success here and there, but had never fully tested the theory in a serious manner. He had heard of miraculous healings due to a person's faith. He knew that the placebo effect was well documented, proving the power of the mind.

This researcher's revelation went well beyond any of that. The implication was that all health lay in a field of information outside of us. The key was in being able to tune into that field. Health, this man claimed, was not generated inside the body in the way that current science understood it to be. Health, it seemed, lay in removing any blockages that prevented people from being able to tune in and receive a clear signal from the quantum field of information—the information field for perfect health.

It gave him pause. He knew that his methods were creating results. He knew that he had helped thousands of patients get off medication, become pain-free, be more mobile, and enjoy a healthy lifestyle by changing their diet. He knew his methods worked. But this information now forced him to reconsider why it worked. Was it possible that the real reason his program worked was because it helped his patients remove the toxins, which allowed their innate wisdom to tune into the field without interference? He didn't yet know what to do with this information.

The speaker went on to explain that what we call hereditary diseases don't have to be written in stone; rather, genes can be switched on and off by their environment. The environment is controlled by a variety of factors, including beliefs. Our beliefs affect our emotions. Emotions can be toxic or supportive. Hereditary illnesses that may express in a toxic environment may remain benign in a healthy environment. Toxins affect the cells' ability to clearly download the information and energy required to thrive. Remove the toxins, and the signal is restored.

While Mark had focused primarily on diet and herbal remedies, the speaker expanded his awareness of other factors impinging on our health. The speaker briefly touched on pesticides, GMOs ,and EMFs, but he focused primarily on the psycho-emotional link to health. For example, someone may be in a neutral situation, but if they believe or feel it is depressing or bad, then their internal environment becomes depressed and negative. As a consequence their cells and DNA will respond as if they are in a negative environment. Conversely, if someone is in a physically negative situation, yet they maintain a positive outlook and believe things are going to work out, then their internal environment remains hopeful and positive. In this case, their cells and DNA respond as if they are in a positive environment. He emphasized repeatedly the power of thoughts to influence health. He went so far as to say that what we believe about our food may be almost as important as the food itself.

The more Mark listened, the more he began to generate a theory. *What if the information in the quantum field is just another word for coding? Everything, including food, has an intrinsic code, but what if we can override that code with our thoughts and reprogram it to be positive instead of negative? Holy smokes, Batman!*

He couldn't believe it. He had already thrown in the towel on his worldview once before, and now it seemed the universe had led him to another crossroads. He must, once again, wrestle with his cognitive dissonance and learn how to hold two opposing paradigms in his mind at the same time.

As he pondered the implications of these concepts, his mind wandered to his time in India. He had heard of the phenomenon of breatharians, people who did not eat at all, but lived purely on life force energy. These pure souls bypassed the need to assimilate nourishment from food. All that they needed for perfect health and energy was provided by this manna from heaven. He had found these stories curious and fascinating, but it had been too far beyond his understanding to give them serious consideration. However, in light of this new information, he finally recognized their significance.

When he came home, he was quieter than usual. Sophie noticed at once and asked him what was going on and if he was okay. He kissed her and reassured her that he was okay, but that he was working something out. She respected his need for space, trusting that he would share his ruminations when he was ready.

It took him a couple days to be able to put his ideas into words. Sophie sat and listened as he explained his theory that everything is energy and information. She contemplated his idea that humans can, in a sense, rewrite the code for health or illness through the power of their minds. It sounded plausible to her.

"Hey, if I can travel through time and space to talk to my former incarnation and heal my issues in real time, then as far as I'm concerned, anything is possible," Sophie contended.

Mark took a lot of comfort in the fact that he could talk to Sophie about these deep, philosophical questions. In the past, when he had tried to discuss similar themes with his friends and colleagues, he had been met with blank stares and disinterest. She was a rare gift, intelligent and intuitive, and he was grateful.

Sophie truly was open to all possibilities, but her conversation with Mark sparked some questions of her own. *If all the information to be healthy, happy, and abundant exists in the quantum field, then why do humans suffer so needlessly and so much? If all of our reality is, at its core, just programming, then why does it seem like the code is inherently corrupt? Why does the default setting seem to be set for pain and suffering? Is it intentional, or a huge cosmic failure?*

She knew there was only one person who could really help her with this. Wendy had mentioned, in an offhanded comment, that she had run across a dark force on her journey into spirituality. Sophie had all but forgotten that she had even mentioned it, but now the memory surfaced.

She called her up on a Saturday morning, so they would have plenty of time to talk uninterrupted. She openly shared her heartache about the plight of the human condition. She didn't have to defend her point of view. Wendy knew Sophie's story. She understood her anger and hurt, not only for herself, but for humanity at large.

"Why does it have to be this way? What's wrong with this world?!" Sophie screamed into the phone.

Wendy knew these existential questions could not be satisfied with a simple or patronizing response. They were questions about the meaning or lack of meaning of life. She understood that these moments must be dealt with gently.

Wendy took a breath and paused before answering. "I agree that there's something wrong with the world, Sophie. I'm not sure it has to be this way, but for reasons that aren't public knowledge, it is this way."

She shared a bit of her worldview at her current stage of evolution. She had adapted her understanding several times over the past couple of years as new information had come to light. It was not easy to share, and she knew it wouldn't be easy to hear. She also knew Sophie was ready for the hard-to-swallow truth.

In Wendy's work with her clients, she focused on healing their subconscious beliefs and programs, helping them resolve abandonment issues and victim mentality, which held them in patterns of self-sabotage and misery. On occasion, she had run into a client for whom her normal tools simply didn't work. Whenever this happened, she started using the resources she had garnered in her spiritual classes. She healed entities and sent them to the light, cut energetic cords and psychic ties and bonds, cleared negative thought forms, and removed etheric implants. In spite of her success with these techniques, she didn't know how these negative influences had come to be and why humans were so vulnerable to their power and control.

She had always found the idea of the devil to be juvenile, a manipulative exploitation by the church to maintain control of the masses. However, the evidence continued to mount that there was indeed a dark force of some kind working against humanity. She wracked her brain as to its motivations. She continued her search until she stumbled upon the most frightening and horrifying idea she had ever encountered.

The more she discovered, the more the lines became blurred between God as taught by religion, and the dark force itself. She contemplated the stories of a god who demanded to be worshipped, who blamed his creation for their flaws, who condemned them to pay for eternity for their transgressions, and who had even ordered genocide in his name. Surely, this couldn't be the real God. But then, who was he? Who were all these people worshipping?

Sophie resonated with most of Wendy's assessments so far. She remembered having the same questions while listening to the preacher when her grandparents had taken her to church. She was tracking so far.

Wendy had concluded that the God of religion was actually a lesser god—the god of this fallen world. The Gnostics had made it clear that a fallen being or dark entity had created the world in which we now live. This Demiurge was not the real God, which she referred to as "prime creator." He was a jealous, insecure being lacking the divine spark. Cut off from his connection to Source, he fed upon the life force energy of the human family.

Because he was jealous of their divinity and authentic ability to feel joy, he had infected the human family with a mind virus of jealousy, self-loathing, and fear. Then, as the father of all narcissists, he used their own empathy and guilt against them, convincing them that it was their fault that they were in this fallen state. He twisted the story to convince them that they were the ones who had betrayed him by seeking knowledge—an infraction for which they deserved punishment and death. Fearing the eternal punishment of hell, humans then had to beg their very perpetrator for forgiveness and mercy. He exploited their misplaced sense of guilt to manipulate them into reincarnating into his world lifetime after lifetime to make recompense for their karma. Essentially, he had created a soul trap. It seemed the Hindus had it mostly right. A soul's true quest was to achieve liberation by overcoming the wheel of samsara.

Wendy couldn't deny the beauty of nature, which seemed to show the hand of a pure and loving creator. There was so much good and so much evil side by side. It was extremely confusing and difficult to sort out.

"Mark's theory about programming and energy vibration actually makes sense to me. It's like good and evil are two different programs running simultaneously. Humans aren't trapped on Earth as a place; they're trapped in a certain vibration, a level of consciousness…" Wendy trailed off, thinking out loud.

"Kind of like a pure creator made a perfect world, a perfect program, and then this other dark being put a layer of dark programming on top of it," Sophie offered.

"Yes, like that!" Wendy exclaimed, working it out in real time. "The Demiurge, or whatever you want to call it, put a virus, like a computer virus, inside the minds of humans."

"It kind of sounds like an AI." Sophie observed, a chill running down her spine. "Which would imply that we're living in a simulation of some kind."

"I didn't want to say it out loud but the thought has crossed my mind," Wendy admitted. "We're living in a simulation, but I think we came from somewhere else."

Sophie was also working it out in real time. In her meditation class, she had been taught that the part of her that resided in Christ consciousness was perfect, untainted by distortion or half-truths, and that the part of us that we're consciously aware of is subject to confusion and lies. That seemed consistent with a perfect program of light and truth and a viral program of darkness and lies.

"What if our higher self is outside the simulation, so to speak, and our conscious self is inside the matrix?" Sophie queried.

"Right?" Wendy started talking excitedly. "Like, what if we chose to come here the same way someone chooses to play a video game, but once we got here, the virtual reality was so immersive and felt so real that we forgot it's just a game?"

"And," Sophie added, keeping the ball rolling, "what if the original game got corrupted with the computer virus that got installed by the the Demiurge?"

Wendy picked up where Sophie left off. "And since artificial intelligence doesn't have real life in the way a soul does, it knows it can only exist inside the simulation. It knows if someone on the outside unplugged the game, it would be destroyed—so it traps human souls inside, like hostages, to prevent its own demise."

"Yeah, and then made up the whole scam about karma and reincarnation to trick souls into staying here of their own free will. The icing on the cake is that it uses the life force energy of us hostages to power the whole operation," Sophie concluded.

They both sat quietly for a moment, digesting the magnitude of what had just poured from their lips.

"Damn, I need a cigarette" Sophie broke the ice, laughing. "Was it good for you?"

Wendy laughed out loud. "Oh ,yeah," she answered in a sultry voice.

"Are we good here? I feel like we're good here," Sophie came back.

"Later, loser."

Sophie mulled over their conversation. *Mind virus. That explains it. People, in their true essence, are good, but they've been corrupted with a mind virus of self-loathing, guilt, and fear.*

She felt a sense of relief, as though she had finally solved a riddle that had been bugging her for years. She was reminded of a quote from Friedrich Nietzsche: "When a matter becomes clear, it ceases to concern you."

Chapter 32

The Whisper

Wendy had given Sophie a lot of food for thought. Some parts made sense. Others were a bit of a stretch. Nevertheless, she wanted to get Mark's take on it. He listened and thought it was as good a theory as any. He agreed that no one could know for sure, but it wasn't really any more far-fetched than other creation stories in circulation.

He was more interested in his particular field of study. He had gone back to the drawing board, attempting to reconcile the new information he had discovered about health being more about tuning into the quantum field than in tangibles like diet and nutrition. When he thought more deeply into it, the lines had begun to blur a couple of years prior.

A friend who was a chiropractor had incorporated kinesiology into his practice. He balanced the body using a form of energy medicine to remove emotional blocks and restore the proper flow of communication between organs, glands, hormones, and the nervous system. Mark had often teased him for being woo-woo. However, when he considered his friend's methods, this new theory was not that big of a leap. Mark was coming to understand that health was less about adding things and more about removing blockages that prevented people from aligning with the truth of their perfect blueprint of health.

Both Sophie and Mark were interested in topics and ideas that could lead humanity into greater freedom and personal sovereignty. Mark focused on guiding people to take control of their physical health, while Sophie focused more on how to overcome the psycho-emotional aspects of human suffering. She was still practicing law, and whenever possible, engaged her clients in deeper conversations about how their conflicts were affecting them personally. They were both advocates for freedom in their own way.

Sophie was no stranger to divorce cases, and the more she spoke intimately with people about the breakdown in their marriage, the more she discovered that they struggled with the same lack of awareness and communication skills that had affected her relationships for so long. They had hired her to win the battle when they had already lost the war. She could feel their pain and see how they had let their egos get in the way of their true heart's desire. It was all rather sad.

She found herself taking on the role of counselor, talking them through the pain of loss and heartbreak. Through this process, on occasion, she was able to guide them towards a reconciliation rather than continuing on the path of divorce. It did not escape the attention of the partners that a disproportionate percentage of her clients dropped their cases. What was good for her clients was in direct conflict with the bottom line.

She started to feel like maybe she had missed her calling. As a young woman determined to be a success both academically and professionally, her career path of law had seemed like the perfect choice. After growing up poor and disadvantaged, it was a way to prove to herself that she was good enough. She had craved the validation it provided, but now outside validation no longer served to fulfill her inner desires. The more she developed her relationship with her inner self, the accolades of others rang hollow. Promotions and recognition were nice, but they didn't give her the sense of purpose they once had.

She finally saw where Wendy was coming from. *Now I get it.* She often found herself lying awake at night, wondering what she wanted to be when she grew up. She chuckled to think of it in those terms. Everything that had seemed so certain before was now uncertain. What had once felt like what she wanted to do, now felt like something she had to do. She felt lost, adrift at sea. *Am I having a midlife crisis?*

Mark listened and offered feedback, but he knew it was a decision only she could make. It was undoubtedly easier to stay with the status quo. She had invested so much time and effort in becoming a lawyer. She knew it inside and out. She was competent and well respected in her field. It was her comfort zone.

Sophie had no clue what she would do if she walked away from law. She just wanted to feel more connected and somehow be involved in helping other people feel more connected too. It was hardly logical, but the feeling persisted. Months went by. She continued to let it sit on the back burner.

Something was stirring inside of her—something unfamiliar yet profound. She found herself questioning the purpose and meaning of everything in life. She looked at the folly of humanity's strivings, the repetitive nature of their conflicts, wars, ambitions, and political debates. Man went round and round, decade after decade, generation after generation, repeating the same patterns with virtually the same outcomes. *It's all so pointless.*

"I think I'm having an existential crisis," she confessed to Mark one day.

"What do you mean?" he asked, genuinely interested.

Sophie explained, as well as she could, the thoughts she had been wrestling with—how humans were constantly doing, yet nothing got done, at least, not in any permanent sort of way. She acknowledged that mankind had made great strides in technology and convenience, but had made little to no progress when it came to the real issues of war or poverty or illness.

"We have better toys, but we're not doing anything better with them. What are we actually doing it for? What's the point of it all?" she said with genuine anguish.

"I get it. I felt exactly the same way when I threw in the towel on Western medicine and went to India," Mark replied empathetically. "I felt like the system was treating patients with one hand and making them sick with the other."

"Look at you, though. You're really doing something good for people. You're helping people take back control of their health. That means something," Sophie contended. "But look at what *I* do. I mean, I help people sue each other—and for what? So they can have more money or get revenge? At the end of the day, I feel like I'm part of the problem, not the solution," she lamented.

"What do you want?" Mark asked bluntly.

"I don't know, but I know it's not this," she replied.

They discussed a way for her to move forward. They agreed she needed some space to clear the air and think. She needed time to sit and let the answers inside of her bubble to the surface without the constant distractions of life's everyday demands. She needed, if only for a little while, to *be* and not do.

So, she arranged to take a leave of absence from work. After considering her options, she booked a bed and breakfast in Sedona for an entire month. It was the perfect getaway, a spiritual Mecca of sorts, complete with hiking, energy vortices, and alternative healing practitioners. Best of all, it was quiet and out of the way, a total change of pace from her normal day-to-day life.

When the day arrived for her trip, she was eager to get on the road. She and Mark had agreed that she would go alone. She needed a total pattern break from anything familiar. This was her opportunity to get to know herself without the fixed self-concept she had adopted and fostered her whole life. This was a chance to be Sophie without the mask of professional, intellectual, friend, daughter, or even wife. She would leave all that behind to discover who and what she was, without props or expectations or preconceived ideas. It was the ultimate adventure.

She was as scared as she was excited. She clung to Mark a little longer than usual as they said their goodbyes. But the farther away she drove, the freer she felt. It was that feeling of driving off into the sunset, no one to answer to, no one to consider but herself, free to do whatever struck her fancy. She could drive as long as she wanted and stop when she wanted and listen to the music she wanted. She couldn't remember there ever being a time when she had felt this unfettered. She breathed it all in and let it out with a sigh.

She hadn't planned ahead where she would spend the night on the way. She wanted to leave everything as open-ended as possible. She would stop when she was too exhausted to keep driving, or when a town or a motel spoke to her. As the sun was setting, she pulled into a nondescript place in a sleepy little town in Oklahoma. She checked in and walked over to a diner for some down-home cooking. Just being able to order whatever guilty pleasure she wanted, without wondering what anyone else thought about it, was freeing in a way she hadn't anticipated. *Just how much of my life have I censored?*

She got the country-fried steak with mashed potatoes, smothered in gravy. Smiling to herself, she felt like she was getting away with something. She savored every delicious, fat-laden bite. But she wasn't done indulging her naughty side, so she ordered a root beer float. She hadn't had one since back when she was in college. Suddenly a wave of self-judgment at her blatant overindulgence swelled up inside of her. She heard that old critical voice—the voice of her mother calling her a "chunky monkey." She caught herself mid-thought. *Screw that. I deserve to live a little.*

She finished up, once again thoroughly relishing the sweet and fizzy experience. She thanked the waitress, leaving her a generous tip. Seeing this middle-aged woman working long and late hours reminded her of how grateful she was for her own life. She took the opportunity to share the wealth and brighten someone else's day.

She made her way back to the motel and settled down in the modest accommodations. She watched some cheesy late-night television reruns, once again enjoying the fact that there was no one else's opinion to consider and no need to adapt her behavior to anyone's expectations. It was a silly, small thing of no consequence, and yet it felt hugely freeing.

* * *

The next day, she was up before the sun rose and pressed on to Sedona. She pulled in just after dark. Everything was as the host had described. She let herself in with the keypad entry, brought in her bags, and unpacked her few things. Not intending to make a steady diet of junk food, she had stopped at the grocery store to pick up some healthy fare more aligned with her goal of becoming clear on all levels. She put her food away, noting that a few spices and basics were already provided.

She walked out on the patio and could hear a fountain in the garden. *Nothing more soothing than the sound of running water.* Noise and light pollution were noticeably absent. She basked in the stillness and the brightness of the stars. *This place is perfect.*

Something about the quiet calm of the space was so immersive that she almost forgot to call Mark and let him know she had made it safely. It was odd how happy she was to be away from everyone, including the love of her life. She hadn't realized how much she had craved this alone time. As soon as they hung up the phone, she fell into a deep, restful sleep.

* * *

She woke up to a view of the red rocks for which Sedona was famous. Hiking to an energy vortex was the first item on her list of things to do. She made a cup of coffee, ate a light breakfast, packed a few snacks, and headed out.

The terrain of the Sonoran Desert was unlike anything she had ever seen. The red rock formations were mesmerizing. At a local visitor center, she was able to pick up a hiking map and get some recommendations for the best places to check out. With two weeks and plenty of time to explore, she chose one of the most popular spots to start. She was a tourist, after all.

Sophie was in good shape these days, so the hike was easy. There wasn't a cloud in the sky. *It's so clear, so blue!* Stopping frequently to admire desert flora that she had never seen before, she climbed to where a vortex was shown on the map. She had made sure to bring plenty of water, so she could stay as long as she liked. She found a spot off the beaten path to sit in solitude. Before long, she found herself deep in meditation.

She didn't know how long she was there. Her consciousness had lifted out of her body and flown over the valley. Lifting higher and higher, like an eagle, she saw the entire landscape. Her spirit wandered back in time, observing a young Native American girl down below her. She felt a connection with this girl, who was living a very different life in a very different time. She watched as she gathered water, walked into a teepee, and made a fire. Sophie marveled at her beauty and grace. She wanted to tell her how beautiful she was. She wondered if she knew.

Then she was standing in front of the girl, looking directly into her eyes. This girl was now observing her, admiring her and wondering if she knew how beautiful *she* was. She walked over to Sophie as if to tell her something, stopping about two feet in front of her. She placed something in her hands and whispered, "Remember."

Sophie woke with a start, surprised to find herself sitting alone high above the valley. Her vision had been so vivid, so real. *Remember,* she repeated to herself. *Remember... Remember what?*

She had not seen what the girl had placed in her hands. She sat for some time, wracking her mind for the details of her encounter. Eventually, she stood up and walked back down the trail to her car, holding tightly onto the image of this girl as if afraid she would disappear forever.

Although she had a strong desire to understand more about what had happened, she recognized that these mysteries were beyond her ability to explore alone. She knew Sedona was a hub for spiritual practitioners of all sorts. Sophie was still in a daze. Her car practically guided itself into the parking lot of a crystal shop. It seemed like the kind of place that would be affiliated with psychics and spiritual advisors. She wasn't wrong. They had a list of mediums, tarot readers, and psychics who worked part-time. She looked at their pictures and read each of their profiles. She felt drawn to one in particular named Elena. Her first availability was the following afternoon. Sophie made an appointment and then bought a couple of crystals recommended by the owner for intuition and protection.

When she spoke to Mark that night, she didn't mention her vision. It felt sacred, a gift for her alone. He caught her up on what was going on back home. He was making some changes at the clinic and incorporating a lot more guided visualization into his patients' protocols. He beamed with pride at the results they were achieving. He had found his calling and loved his life. He missed Sophie terribly, of course, but he was so happy that she was following her inner guidance and finding her true path.

"You're my angel," Sophie said, surprised to hear that word come out of her mouth. She meant it though. He was the best person she knew. He was a gift to everyone who had the privilege of being in his presence. She knew the world was brighter just for having him in it. He was her everything—her anchor, her rock, her cheerleader, and her lover. It was because of him that she was able to feel both safe enough and free enough to embark on this adventure of self-discovery.

"I love you. Deeply." She said, and hung up the phone.

Chapter 33

Dark Night of the Soul

Sophie couldn't wait until her appointment with Elena. She had so many questions, and in general, she was extremely curious about getting a reading. When she returned to the crystal shop, she was ushered through a doorway with hippie beads and motioned to sit at a small, round table.

Elena was one of those rare psychics who didn't ask a lot of questions. She preferred to listen to her guides and get her information directly from Spirit.

"There's a woman here," Elena started.

Sophie was excited. She was sure it was the girl from her vision.

Elena continued, "She says you are a bright light from beyond time and space. You are here to help others remember who they are. Don't forget where you came from and where you're going. You are one with God, everywhere and everywhen."

Sophie couldn't tell if this was the Native American girl who was speaking or not. She had used the word "remember." *Remember who I am,* she repeated in her mind.

Elena cocked her head sideways as if there was a shift in the energy. "She's saying thank you. Thank you for reminding her of who she was. She's saying don't worry, he's okay. He's with me now. He's always been with both of us."

Elena opened her eyes and stared intently at Sophie.

The message did not sound at all like it was from the Native American girl she had seen. *What a strange message? Are psychics always this cryptic?*

Elena could tell from the look on her face that she was confused and not a little disappointed. She explained that, while she was the messenger, she was not always privy to the full context and meaning of the message. She offered that the woman had looked like she was from an earlier time period and wore a long dress to the floor.

Sophie instantly recognized this as her former incarnation from her past life regression. She was stunned. *I helped her remember who she was?* she pondered. But w*ho is the man she was referring to?*

Elena had nothing to offer about the specifics but told Sophie that it would likely be revealed in the coming days.

Sophie was glad she had recorded the session so she could review it later. *"A bright light from beyond time and space,"* She played it over in her mind. It all sounded rather mystical and woo-woo. The cynical side of her wondered if the psychic gave everyone these types of sweeping, grandiose messages. *It was hardly specific.*

She had left her phone in the car to guarantee no interruptions during her session. She was surprised to see she had three missed calls from Mark's mother. *That's weird. She hardly ever calls me.*

She was still processing the session, so decided to wait until she got back to her room before calling her mother-in-law back. She didn't know it yet, but her trip was about to be cut short.

She sat down on the couch and listened to the voice message. There was an urgency in Miranda's voice, and she said to call her right away. Sophie felt a surge of adrenaline flow upwards through her spine, putting her on high alert. She pulled up Miranda's number and hit the green call button on her phone.

As soon as Miranda started to talk, Sophie felt the blood drain out of her face and turn to ice in her veins.

"Are you there?" Miranda asked. "Sophie, can you hear me?"

Sophie sat dumbly, unable to speak. Her whole world had fallen out beneath her. Her hands began to shake.

"I'm here," she finally replied. "Is he okay? He has to be okay."

"He's in critical condition. The doctors can't guarantee anything. It's very serious. You need to come home right away," Miranda said directly. "I'm so sorry," she added, sobbing.

"I'll be there as soon as I can," Sophie told her. "I'll figure out how to get there as soon as I can."

She hung up the phone. She was in a full fight-or-flight response. Mark had been in a car accident on his way to work. His car had been T-boned on the driver's side in the intersection just two blocks from his office. The other driver, going ninety in a forty-five-mile-per-hour zone, had blown past a red light and right into Mark's car. It only took minutes for the paramedics to arrive. They had removed Mark, unconscious, from the vehicle and driven him, with lights and sirens, to the nearest trauma center.

The emergency personnel had initiated a full trauma activation. The surgical team had descended upon him, evaluating him from head to toe. First things first: he was intubated to protect his airway and ensure that his brain was sufficiently oxygenated. A CAT scan had revealed a ruptured spleen. He was rushed to surgery and later taken to the trauma ICU, still in a coma.

After Sophie recovered from the initial shock, she went into action mode. This wasn't the time to fall apart. She could do that later. Right now, she needed to figure out how to get home the fastest way possible. Sedona was a relatively remote location. Flagstaff, an hour away, was the closest major airport. But what was she to do with her car? Driving back would take her twenty-four hours if she drove straight through. That option was neither safe nor efficient. She decided to leave her car in long-term parking. She would have to figure out how to retrieve it after the dust had settled.

She got online and booked the next available flight. She would have to change planes in Denver. She packed up her stuff, which was fortunately minimal, and texted the host of the bed and breakfast to let him know what was going on. In literally minutes, she was on her way to Flagstaff. Her only thought, circling round and round in her brain, was *Please, God, let him be okay.*

She found the remote parking lot and took the shuttle to the terminal. She checked her bags and made her way through security. There was still a two-hour wait until boarding. She didn't watch anything on her phone. She didn't read a book. She sat motionless, silently repeating her mantra. *Please, God, let him be okay.*

Caught in the limbo of timelessness, she waited. Reliably and predictably, the hands of the clock inched forward, second by second, minute by minute, until at last she found herself seated on the plane. *Finally. Please, God, let him be okay.*

Like an automaton, she shuffled through the motions of deboarding, lining up, reboarding and taking off for the final leg of her journey. Mark's father picked her up from the airport. Gone was his usual cheery disposition. His face was expressionless, his affect flat. The prospect of losing his son had clearly sent him into a state of shock. He didn't speak, except to update her on Mark's condition. "Unchanged" was all he said.

They drove in silence to the hospital. He parked. She followed him to the ICU.

The moment she saw Mark was when she finally broke down. Miranda and Pete remained in the hall, giving Sophie time to be alone with him. Tears streamed down her face as she touched his face and stroked his hair. She held his hand in hers, kissing the back of it. She leaned in to place her cheek against his. Sobs racked her small frame as grief overtook her.

After an hour or so, his parents walked back into the room. They tearfully hugged each other. It was comforting to know that they shared a love for this beautiful soul, whom she called husband and they called son. It was a bond that would help to fill the void in their hearts as they moved into the future.

Mark's spirit hung on for three more days, giving Sophie and his parents time to come to terms with the inevitable. It was a small mercy. Mark had done so much good in his short lifetime. He had shown Sophie a love she had never known. He had touched the lives of so many patients. He had honored his parents while being true to himself. He was, perhaps, too good for this world.

They all sat by his side around the clock, taking turns to go home, shower, or nap for an hour or two. Sophie and Miranda were there when his spirit left him. The heart monitor flatlined. A team of responders rushed into the room and began resuscitation measures.

After a moment or two, Miranda quietly said, "Let him go."

They called the code, and the doctor pronounced, "Time of death: one thirteen pm."

More tears and sobs ensued. Sophie knew letting him go was the right thing to do. He had fought the good fight, and she knew somewhere deep down that he had completed what he had come here to do.

The nurse asked Sophie about the necessary details of where his body was to be sent and whether they had picked out a funeral home. No one had allowed themselves to think this far ahead. Sophie was grateful for Miranda's strength and guidance with all the details and planning that followed. At the time when one is at their lowest, wanting nothing more than to lie in the fetal position and grieve, they are called upon to take care of the thousand details that follow on the heels of a loved one's death. But still, these things could not be avoided.

The next few days were a whirlwind of calls, planning, services and arrangements. Miranda took on the lion's share of the responsibility. She had always been an example of grace under pressure, a trait she had passed on to her son. Sophie was grateful to be a part of his family, to witness the origin of his legacy. It was grounding, and it was good. She belonged.

Of all the calls she had to make, there was only one person Sophie actually wanted to talk to.

When Wendy answered the phone, she could not understand anything Sophie was saying through the sobs and cries.

"What's going on?" Wendy asked.

"He's… He's… He's gone," was all Sophie was able to get out.

"Who's gone? What happened?!" Wendy asked.

It took Sophie a full minute to slow her weeping enough to tell her the story. Wendy couldn't believe it. Mark had been so young and vibrant, so in love with life and with Sophie. Wendy didn't try to offer her some pat answer or cliché response. She knew this was real, and it was raw. She simply sat on the phone with Sophie and let her cry. Every couple minutes, she quietly reminded her, "I'm here. I'm here. Anything you need, I'm here."

Wendy cleared her calendar and went to be with Sophie. She was there by her side for the funeral. She was there sitting on the bed when Sophie needed to talk or not talk. She made her meals, did her dishes, and took care of everything she could. When it was all over, they discussed the best plan to retrieve her car from Flagstaff.

The death of Sophie's most beloved did not permit her to stop living or doing what needed to be done. The world continued to spin on its axis, and she must continue to move forward. She longed to be with Mark, wherever he was. She imagined it must be better than this place, if only because he was there. It wasn't that she was suicidal, she just no longer wanted to be here. Life was empty without him. There was no joy. She went through the motions, detached from a sense of purpose. All was meaningless.

Wendy recognized Sophie's state. She had been through something similar, albeit much less intense, when she had had her heart broken by Manny, years before. Prior to her relationship with him, she'd thought she had everything figured out. She thought she knew what she wanted and knew how to get it. The world was her oyster. But when Manny left her, and there was nothing she could do to win him back, her world and her identity crumbled. In that moment, nothing made sense anymore. It was a dark place to be— so dark that it was impossible to imagine the light would ever reappear. But eventually it had, and life had taken on a richer, deeper meaning than she had been able to conceive of before.

Wendy was a wise soul. She knew only time and self-reflection could heal Sophie's near-fatal wound. There were no magic words or philosophical interpretations that could reach or soothe those places that were hurting. But she could be there as a healing presence, a port in the storm.

Wendy booked their flights to Flagstaff for the following week. They would take their time driving back, stopping whenever and wherever it felt intuitive to do so. She downloaded some comedy movies to watch on the plane. She thought it might be helpful for Sophie to watch something mindless and silly to get her mind off of everything. Anything that might boost her serotonin levels, even briefly, would be beneficial.

She chose a couple movies that they had watched together when Sophie had visited her in California, hoping they might be an anchor to better times. It worked. Movies can be hypnotic in nature. They draw us into another world and engage our emotions as if we were part of the story. It was the perfect reprieve from the recent tragedy. Several times during the flight, she saw Sophie giggling. It was good to see her smile and laugh again.

After landing, they retrieved the car without a hitch. Wendy was almost surprised that things had gone as expected, relieved that there hadn't been a glitch in the matrix. They decided to get a few miles under their belt before packing it in for the night.

They were about to start heading east when Sophie said, "You know, we really should see the Grand Canyon."

Wendy immediately pulled onto the shoulder. "We really should!" she exclaimed with a smile. "Oh my god, we're going to have a real adventure!"

Sitting right there on the side of the road, they figured out a game plan. They found an available room for the night and headed that way. A lightness entered the car. Hope piggybacked its way onto the expectancy of surprise making a tiny opening in the dark clouds of Sophie's mind.

* * *

The next morning, they embarked on an exploration of the sights. When she stood next to the gaping chasm, Sophie was struck with her smallness. The grandness of this canyon, by its very size, instantly put her life into perspective. She, and all that was implied by her existence, including her problems, were insignificant compared to its greatness. The span of her life was infinitesimal in comparison with the timelessness of this gorge, which had been carved out over millions of years.

The history of mankind ran like a time-lapse movie before her eyes. She saw people being born, living, and dying a thousand deaths. She knew that she herself had lived many lifetimes, knowing joy, love, and heartbreak in each of them. She saw at once the insignificance and magnificence of it all. Like this river in the canyon, she was ever changing and yet ever the same. As her small, separate self, she was a tiny drop in the ocean. But as one with the all, she was as vast as the ocean itself.

She stood there, taking it all in. Gaia was communing with her without words, her wisdom imparting a truth that could be felt, but never understood; known, but never explained. She knew in that moment that everything was okay. It had always been okay. In fact, it was perfect.

"I feel him here," she said when Wendy walked up to her.

"Yeah," was all Wendy replied, nodding her head.

They stood together. The wind kicked up, blowing their hair in their faces and flapping their clothes against their bodies. It was with some effort that they made their way back to the car.

"Wow, that came out of nowhere," Wendy said.

"I suspect it came out of somewhere." Sophie smiled.

Wendy smiled back. "The winds of change."

They were both satisfied with their excursion and decided to get back on the road. The day was already half gone, so they only made it as far as Albuquerque.

About two hours into the trip, Sophie said, "I should have been there. I shouldn't have gone to Sedona."

Wendy knew survivor's guilt and remorse were a natural part of the grieving process. She waited a minute before responding.

"Mark knew what he was doing, Soph. Our entrance and exit are decided on a soul level. We can't wrap our minds around, it and it doesn't seem fair by our ego understanding, but you can trust that his soul chose this. It was never up to you. There was nothing you could do or should have done about it. There was nothing he, from his ego perspective, could do about it either. Forgive him, and forgive yourself, because there was never anything to forgive. He loved you. That's what's real, now and always. Hold onto that."

It felt like a déjà vu moment. *All is forgiven. There was never anything to forgive.* Somewhere in time, she had heard those words before.

Sophie felt the truth of Wendy's words. Mark had loved her. She had never doubted it for a second. He had made sure she felt his love for her. His love had healed so much hurt and heartache in her. His love had restored her belief in herself and her knowing that she was worthy. He was the best thing that had ever happened to her ,and she would be forever grateful. *Thank you, baby.*

"They're right. It truly is better to have loved and lost than never to have loved at all," Sophie said after riding for a couple of hours in silence.

"Yes, it truly is," Wendy agreed.

"I just miss him… so much," Sophie reflected.

"I know," Wendy said quietly.

They rode on in silence for another half hour. Wendy turned on a streaming radio station, and they listened to the songs they had loved in college. Sophie looked out the window, every now and then singing a few bars of a favorite chorus. They pulled into a hotel, ate dinner, and crashed early, with plans to get an early start the next morning.

Sophie lay in bed, her thoughts swirling. So much had happened in the last two weeks. It was surreal. It seemed impossible that Mark was really gone. Death was strange, so final. She drifted off to sleep dreaming that he was lying beside her. *I love you, baby. I miss you.*

* * *

It took them four days to make the trip, twice as long as when Sophie had driven to Sedona. They stopped at a few of the attractions and national parks along the way. Wendy never made her feel rushed or like she was in a hurry to get back to her own life. She was fully present.

Sophie was so grateful for Wendy. It was rare to have a friend who showed up the way she did. Sophie was blessed to have someone who could help her navigate the difficult emotional and spiritual turmoil that arises in death. With Wendy's wisdom and gentle presence, she was able to negotiate these waters, remaining anchored in the truth of who she was as an eternal, divine being. Wendy helped her see things from a higher perspective, without getting lost in the pain.

When Sophie dropped her off at the airport, she gave her the longest hug she had ever given anyone. All she said was "Thank you" as she looked into her eyes. She didn't need to say more. They both knew. She was her soul sister, and they were on this journey together, forever. Sophie watched until she had made it through security.

Chapter 34

Madeleine's Redemption

An oppressive cloud of guilt clung to Madeleine like the stench of a rotting carcass. It permeated everything she did. Every line of her face, curve of her body, word, and step was laced with it. If she could have ended her life, she would have. It was only her responsibility and love for Steffan that prevented her from doing so.

Steffan was growing up. It was becoming unsuitable for him to live in the brothel any longer. The madam put him to work with odd jobs and general upkeep, but he was getting to an age where he needed to choose his own life path. He decided to seek out a carpenter apprenticeship.

After getting advice from several of the regular patrons of the madam's establishment, he found a master craftsman with a cheerful disposition and fair business practices. He had heard the horror stories of countless young men who were severely mistreated, yet unable to break the contract of their indentureship. He wished to learn a trade and was willing to serve his mentor in exchange for his training, but he would be no man's slave. He ended up making a suitable and agreeable arrangement. He would be living with the carpenter's family and receive room and board in exchange for his service. He would be allowed to visit his mother on Sundays. The rest of the week, he would be at his mentor's beck and call.

With Steffan otherwise situated, Madeleine found herself in a new energetic space. She no longer felt the constraint and burden of being responsible for his care. She knew he loved her, and it would be difficult for him if something happened to her, but she also knew that he was going to be okay. He was his own person now, independent, capable of surviving with-out her.

Without the distraction and purpose of providing for Steffan, she finally came face to face with herself. She was no longer able to compartmentalize the guilt over what she had done. She had to, at last, come to grips with the horror of her betrayal of Chelsea. It had never gone away. It had always been in the secret recesses and corners of her mind. Now it came back with a raging vengeance, as if it had just happened the day before.

She took to drinking—not because it helped, but because she didn't have a reason not to. It was a way to punish herself, though she knew there was nothing that could absolve her of her guilt. She added whiskey to her coffee in the morning and ended the day with a nightcap. She honestly didn't know why she hadn't taken her own life. Maybe one day she would imbibe enough liquid courage to get the job done.

It was an afternoon in spring that she found herself wandering in the woods. She hadn't set out to go anywhere in particular. She had just started walking, following her feet wherever they took her. As she meandered along a path, stepping in and out of the dappled sunlight, she heard a whisper in the trees. She couldn't make out what it said, but it sounded like the voice of a woman. Quite unexpectedly, she discovered that she was in the old clearing where the gatherings had once been held.

The wind swirled around her. She felt a presence. Her instincts told her to run from this godforsaken place, but something held her feet to the ground. She stood still. A mixture of nostalgia, wonder, and guilt welled up in her. Being at those gatherings had been the best experience of her life, but what had happened as a result had been the worst. Her body felt weak. She slipped to her knees. She felt as if she were once again kneeling before Chelsea, begging for forgiveness.

Then strangely, she sensed a subtle presence. It was a loving presence, and she felt a warmth as if being hugged from the inside.

Inside her mind, she heard the words, "*All is forgiven. I'm here with you. You are not alone.*" She felt a female presence, reminiscent of the sisterhood she had once been a part of, a presence from beyond this time and place. The voice, though not external, was undeniably clear. Most of all, it filled her with a sense of comfort she had not known for many years.

Tears rolled down her cheeks. Chelsea, all those years ago, had told her she was forgiven, that there was never anything to forgive. But Madeleine had been unable to receive absolution, because she had never been able to forgive herself. Guilt is an exacting and merciless oppressor, impossible to appease, its demands never satisfied. One may give their whole life to make amends, and it will never be enough. Madeleine had lived this way, in the grip of guilt's chokehold, as it insatiably extracted her life force as penance for her sins.

She saw, in her mind's eye, a woman standing in front of her. She did not recognize her physical features or the type of clothes she was wearing, but she felt a kinship as though she knew her somehow. The woman smiled and walked over to her. She put her arms around her, and as she did so, Madeleine was filled with more joy and peace than she had ever known. This other woman hugged her, and she disappeared into her as though she was a part of her—as though she was her.

For the first time since it had happened, she allowed herself to feel love. She could not have resisted the comfort of this female presence if she had tried. Divine love is more powerful than fear. Her guilt melted in its pure presence. She stood in the truth of her innocence. She was whole.

An opening was created in her consciousness. This other self had allowed her to feel the overwhelming truth of love that dissolves all distortion and confusion. Suddenly, she saw things clearly that, prior to that moment, had been obscured. This other self showed her that she was more than she had supposed herself to be, and that life was so much more than it appeared.

In that moment, Madeleine knew that Chelsea had continued on, that she had never truly died, but had simply changed forms. Her spirit was unharmed and unscathed by all that had happened. She saw now that suffering, even unto death, is an illusion. She knew, without knowing how she knew, that life is fleeting, but souls are eternal. She understood that, similar to childbirth, the pain is soon forgotten, but the gift remains. All of it had been designed for her soul's evolution. Souls came here to know themselves as divine creators under the direst of circumstances. It was the ultimate test of overcoming.

The only thing that's real is us. The rest is a dream, albeit a dream of epic proportions. How can someone be condemned for what they are dreaming? With crystal clarity, she saw it. There truly was never anything to forgive.

She wanted to run and proclaim the good news, to shout from the rooftops and announce in the square that she was free, and that all men were free. She tempered her excitement with discernment. The wisdom of years had taught her that most people were not ready for an idea this big. Most people were entrenched in their suffering, in love with the drama of their victim stories. Many are called but few are chosen.

For too long, she had remained disconnected from Spirit. As she lay there on the grass in the clearing, basking in the warmth of the sun, she promised herself that she would rekindle her connection with Spirit and her higher self. It was the only real thing in life. In that moment, she decided never to take anything in the material world too seriously ever again. She saw the trappings of life for what they were: transitory waves on the ocean of eternity. She could ride them or avoid, them but never again would she allow herself to be engulfed by them.

Rather than running and shouting from the rooftops, she decided she would quietly share, with those souls who were ready, the truth of their innocence and the eternal nature of their divine self. She would show them, as she had been shown, through the power of love.

When the sun was low on the horizon, Madeleine made her way back to her residence. There was a lightness of being and a spring in her step. She sang in chorus with the birds as she had not done since back when her mother was alive. She felt as if she had been reborn anew.

She arrived at the brothel at dusk. Several girls rushed over to her, excitedly wanting to share the news.

"He's here. He's back. He's come for you!" they all said in unison.

Madeleine barely had time to wonder what they were talking about before he appeared.

"Good evening, Madeleine."

"Mr. Giles. What a surprise," Madeleine responded, slightly breathless.

"May I talk to you? Alone?" he asked.

"Yes, of course," she replied.

The girls were right. He had come for her. He explained that his wife had suffered a severe illness. Despite all efforts on the part of the physicians, she had at last succumbed to it.

"She is dead now." he said solemnly.

"I am so sorry," Madeleine replied sincerely.

"Yes, thank you," he acknowledged.

He went on to explain that he had remained faithful in his duties as a father. He had comforted and supported his children through the grief of losing their mother.

"I really am so very sorry," was all Sophie knew to say.

"Thank you." He replied. "I have observed the proper mourning period, Madeleine. I'm sure you are not surprised, my situation now changed, that my thoughts have returned to you."

Madeleine touched his hand and looked deep into his eyes. She did not respond.

"I'm sorry for the way I left. I know leaving suddenly without saying goodbye was cowardly and unkind," he went on.

"I understood," she offered.

"If you can find it in your heart to forgive me, I would like to make it up to you."

A smile broke across her face. "Are you saying you want to make an honest woman of me?" she teased. "What will all those genteel folk of polite society say, Mr. Giles?"

"Polite society be damned," he blurted out. "I've spent my whole life conforming to their rules and expectations, and it hasn't brought me one iota of happiness. I want to be with you, Madeleine. You're the only one I care about. Will you have me?" he pleaded.

"I will, sir," she said quietly. "I will have you. I've always been yours."

He had tears in his eyes as he grabbed her in his arms. "I'll never let you go."

"I know." Madeleine did know, in a way she could not have known before that day, that they had always been together.

Chapter 35

Transcendence

It's strange pretending to return to normal life after the death of your true love. Nothing, of course, is normal at all. Sophie extended her leave of absence. The loss of Mark had exacerbated her midlife crisis. When she had left for Sedona, she had been questioning her life choices and whether she wanted to continue to live her life based on outdated values and ambitions. In the aftermath of his death, she was questioning all of that and so much more.

Her mind wandered in so many directions. Mark had shown her, by his example, that life was about being rather than doing. It was his spirit, his essence, that had touched the lives of friends, family, and patients. She understood now that it's not our accomplishments that give our lives meaning; it's who we are. She knew that Mark had been a light in the darkness, no matter where he was or what he was doing. There was no need to force anything, no need to push, no need to contrive a life of purpose. His spirit, his essence, was what had given his actions and his life purpose.

She spent the next few weeks in the crucible. Old ideas, constructs, and ways of being were burned away, layer after layer, painful at times, liberating at others. She gave herself enough time to disengage from all that was familiar so as to allow something new to emerge.

Her whole life, she had been on her way somewhere—on her way to becoming valedictorian, on her way to graduating law school with honors, on her way to being a successful lawyer, on her way to being made partner at the firm. She had taken on these roles and ambitions, imagining that they were her true identity, without ever considering that one day, all of it would come to a complete and full stop.

Mark's death had woken her up to the fleeting nature of life. She knew for certain that she would see Mark again, that he lived on. Her connection with him was something real and lasting. She became keenly aware that while souls will live forever, one's worldly achievements will wither and fade away, forgotten and insignificant.

With all the jostling of her thoughts, one question emerged. It surfaced over and over again. She could not evade it. *Who am I really?*

Her mind swirled in a flurry of memories. She remembered, as a small child, the love she had felt when her mother had wanted to spend time with her, cuddling her. She remembered the heartache of when she had been tossed aside and ignored. She remembered the way the water felt on her skin in the bathtub, warm and delicious. She remembered her wonder at the beauty of the trees and the sky. She remembered the intensity of desire and rejection through so many of her relationships with men. She relived the exquisite pleasure and pain of all of it.

In each moment of her life, it had felt as if the whole of her existence was consumed with the emotion of that solitary experience. In the bad times, the pain of self-rejection and abandonment had consumed her, blotting out the existence of anything else. Now, with death as her teacher, she could see that the entire experience of life was transitory, as illusory as a dream. Nothing about it was real except the souls themselves. And nothing mattered, nothing meant anything except the wisdom those same souls attained from their experiences.

She herself had been completely beguiled by the convincing nature of this reality. It had felt so real. It still felt real in many ways. As long as she remained in her avatar body, she would be subject to pain and pleasure, joy and sadness. But with her new understanding of the true nature of reality, she could weather life's storms and enjoy life's gifts without attachment or resistance. Those things didn't mean anything. She was the only thing that was real.

She breathed a sigh of relief, like that of coming home after a long and difficult journey. The Buddha's wise philosophy of nonattachment and nonresistance echoed in her mind. She smiled to herself. *He was onto something.*

Tethered to her higher self, she would stay grounded in the truth of eternal love and perfection. One could, it seemed, be in the world, but not of it.

Her mind turned to Wendy and Mark, beautiful souls who had been her sojourners, guiding her lovingly into the truth of who she was. Images of the woman she had encountered in her past life regression, the vision of the Native American woman in the hills of Sedona, and the message that had come through Elena all flooded her consciousness. An awareness began to surface—a realization that she was all of them and none of them. In each moment, she had taken on a different identity, yet beneath all of them, she had remained the same.

There was a consciousness that ran through each of her identities—a consciousness that was always changing and yet ever unchanged, a consciousness that ran through all things. Just as it expressed through her personal experiences with limitless variety, so too it expressed through all life with boundless variety and creativity. All of her pain and joy and love and heartbreak was part of the ride. It was terrible and wonderful and confusing and transcendent.

It all became so clear. She was a part of the one consciousness on its way to knowing its Infinite Self. She was part of a beautiful symphony, playing her individual instrument while coalescing with the music of all life, interchangeably taking on the roles of composer, conductor, musician, and audience. In any moment, she was one, and yet in every moment, she was all.

She had come here to know herself as an infinite expression of the All. In the process, she would assist others in awakening to their divinity, in the same way that Mark and Wendy had been the way-showers for her. One could not know themselves to be the light unless they faced and overcame the shadow. She had done that. And it was in that moment that Sophie remembered.

I am the light of consciousness.

9 798904 175993